Albert Lauterbach is Chairman of the Social Science Faculty at Sarah Lawrence College, and was educated at the University of Vienna in the period between the two world wars.

Economic Security

AND

Individual Freedom

Can we have both?

By Albert Lauterbach

Cornell University Press

ITHACA, NEW YORK, 1948

Copyright 1948 by Cornell University

Cornell University Press

London: Geoffrey Cumberlege

Oxford University Press

PRINTED IN THE UNITED STATES OF AMERICA BY THE
VAIL-BALLOU PRESS, INC., BINGHAMTON, NEW YORK

Contents

Contents

iv

Economic Security and Individual Freedom

Can We Have Both?

CHAPTER I

The Two Fears: Oppression and Depression

THE ORDEAL of the second world war in a generation has been over for a time, but real peace is far away. A shattered civilization, still plagued by hunger, exhaustion, and hatred, is trying to rise from the ruins and to take stock of the physical and moral destruction wrought. It also begins to search for the real causes of a machine age's running amuck, and of the disastrous interplay of war and misery in the twentieth century. The stakes in this search are high. Unless a repetition on a larger scale of mass despair and national frustration can be prevented, mankind is heading for more depressions and more wars. The specter of the atomic bomb has joined that of bankruptcy and mass unemployment in making every nation and every class insecure and restless.

What has prevented western man from setting an end to his plight and that of mankind? What in particular has made him shrink from controlling the forces that have led to periodic slumps in all capitalist and some other countries for well over a century? Until recently it was chiefly the belief that depressions could as little be controlled as the yellow fever, for instance, and that any attempt at control could do only harm. Today yellow fever has been conquered, but depressions have not—or only at a price that a free man is unwilling to pay. The fear that by bringing material misery under control we might jump from the frying pan into the fire, and that the inevitable price for economic security is political oppression, accounts for the resigned acceptance by many of unemployment as a permanent or periodic occurrence.

Yet if there is one obvious lesson from the disastrous thirties, it is that economic chaos has a deadly effect upon freedom and peace alike. Millions of unemployed workers, bankrupt merchants, and farmers in debt after the crash of 1929 became the easy prey of Nazi demagogues in Germany. Propaganda financed by a short-sighted but powerful clique of Ruhr industrialists and eastern Junkers succeeded in diverting the wrath of many victims of the depression from the deeper economic causes to the parties and institutions of democracy. Inflated promises of booming business and high employment, playing upon the popular feeling that a change in regime could not possibly make things worse and might perhaps make them better, gave the Nazis the mass support they needed. It also helped them in converting the latent nationalism of many into a cocky bid for arms and *Lebensraum*.

More than any other single factor, therefore, economic insecurity contributed, after 1929, to Germany's drift into totalitarian organization for armed aggression. In Italy and Japan prolonged misery had a similar share at various times in the mass support for a strong hand at home and expansion abroad. Nations with older democratic traditions managed to retain their sanity despite a comparable disruption of economic life, but one shudders at the probable narrowness of the margin in some of them, too.

The illusion that past conditions were a model of normality easily arises in the midst of turmoil. Yet every war, with its aftermath, is part of a society in flux, even though war usually involves the temporary adoption of more rapid, violent, and cruel methods than are ordinarily employed in the never-ending process of social change.

The problems implied in a return to real peace are further obscured by the traditional lag of phraseology behind action. Some people speak of the period before 1941, or before 1933, in terms of perfect freedom of enterprise. They imply that all the recent controls over economic life have been bureaucratic extravagancies. Still others think of government regulations in terms of politics rather than economics, and are not so much worried about the regulations as such as about the political group that happens to administer them.

3

Actually the American economy during the interwar period was a mixed economy even before the rise of the New Deal. In the United States as elsewhere interstate commerce and international trade were reaching out; industry was being concentrated financially and technologically; the price structure was becoming rigid; monopolistic abuses were affecting the interests of millions; business fluctuations were showing an increased social impact; and the influence of the labor movement was growing. These conditions had led to numerous measures of social legislation, to government agencies in the economic field, and to a substantial amount of public works and property. As a result of the great depression this trend toward governmental intervention was greatly accelerated.

On top of this, social control of business expanded enormously during the Second World War. The war demonstrated how quickly full employment could be achieved, and it caused national production to rise far beyond what had been believed to be its practical limit. One price for this achievement, it is true, was a growth of the national debt that caused some of us sleepless nights. The future role of public spending remains a controversial question to be sure; but after the recent experiences with full employment, increased production, and rising incomes, few of us would be willing to acquiesce once more in an economy of underemployment, underproduction, and underconsumption.

Most of us now regard full employment, huge production, high consumption, and social security as indispensable features of a sound peace economy, and as long-range goals of a responsible policy. The purpose of this study is to show not only that political and cultural freedom is compatible with such goals of economic policy, but that the most dangerous foes of freedom are insecurity and misery, especially after a great national effort in the wake of a total war.

Chaos Versus Freedom

There is considerable opposition today to any organized prevention or flattening of periodic slumps, the core of most programs for social control or economic planning in the western world. Such opposition, which is frequently, though inexactly, identified with a conservative philosophy of society, has two possible roots.

The first is the fear of individuals or groups now in a privileged position that such planning might affect their vested interests. This category includes potentially the stockholders of corporations whose profits or dividends might be adversely affected by government controls or a continuous seller's market for labor, or of corporations whose property might be taken over by public bodies. Stockholders who belong to the anxious type fear straight confiscation, while others dislike the idea of having their shares replaced by low-interest public bonds. The privileged group also includes persons in high managerial positions. Their income and power might be reduced as a result of the requirements of economic planning, or they might have to look for less attractive jobs. Especially is this true of those who have not risen to corporation presidencies the hard way from the proverbial newsboy's job, but who picked the right kind of parents and inherited wealth and influence from them.

To argue with this first type of critics is not too fruitful. It is easy to understand their personal unwillingness to step down from their lofty heights; but it is also essential to call their bluff as soon as they try to translate their special interests into general principles of social behavior. Whenever they candidly admit that social control of economic life might interfere with their way of life and that they will therefore fight it to the very last, they deserve at least the respect due to intellectual honesty. But when they try to talk other groups of citizens out of preventing misery on the ground that this would do as much harm to society in general as it would to their own privileges, then they must expect to see such propaganda exposed for what it is.

The second group of critics deserves not only respect but a painstaking investigation of its apprehensions. This group abhors social control because it sincerely and ardently believes that such a policy inevitably involves regimentation and, in the last resort, a totalitarian oppression of the individual. In the United States the attitude of this group toward social control or economic planning is often based on a historical mythology which runs somewhat like this:

"Free competition is the only economic system that is compatible with freedom. Capitalism and democracy are practically synonymous concepts in their social meaning and are like Siamese twins in practice: capitalist enterprise cannot live without democracy; democracy cannot exist without capitalism. America has grown up as a free country because it believed from the outset in private enterprise, competition, and individualism. Many other nations, however, have succumbed to economic regimentation and thus inevitably sacrificed their political liberties as well.

"The former Axis nations, in particular, let their free enterprise be swept away by a steadily growing bureaucracy which eventually culminated in a totalitarian dictatorship. Labor and socialist movements, whether in their red or in their pink varieties, through their anticapitalist propaganda indirectly helped undermine the popular belief in freedom. It was more or less accidental that the Nazis or Fascists, rather than the Reds or Pinks, managed to seize power and to establish their particular brand of totalitarianism. The difference between them was chiefly in the color of their shirts anyway.

"In the United States, too, there are supporters of a bureaucratic regimentation, which, in its last consequences, would lead to a socialistic totalitarianism. The chief danger is in an alliance of bureaucrats, who are driven by an insatiable lust for power, and long-haired crackpots, who have never met a payroll. Their combined influence has already been strong enough to ruin

7

our past prosperity and to endanger our freedoms. Nothing in the least is the matter with free enterprise so long as it is left alone, and social control or planning is one of those catchwords that have elsewhere helped destroy capitalism, democracy, and freedom."

Is there need to emphasize the quotation marks into which the preceding three paragraphs have been put? Possibly they should be as tall as the Empire State Building, for the notions summarized in these paragraphs are as frequent as they are cockeyed. They are based above all on a distortion of history—both American and foreign—that in itself has far more in common with totalitarian than with democratic methods of historiography and education.

Democracy and Capitalism: The Historical Record

In the first place, America has not always been a capitalist democracy. At the time of the Declaration of Independence, America was a nation of pioneering farmers and craftsmen, with elements of feudalism in the South and some other areas, and with a class of slaves at the bottom of the social scale. Only some eighty years ago did slavery disappear and the rapid development of modern industrial capitalism get under way. The magnificent ideas of the Bill of Rights were based on the heritage of the Enlightenment Period in western Europe rather than on any rapid advance of industrial technology and large-scale enterprise, which came almost a century later. Besides, there have been many scattered elements of social and economic planning, especially on the local scale, in the historical development of North America ever since its settlement.[1]

There is nothing in American tradition that would necessarily link freedom or democracy with the business principles of John D. Rockefeller, Sr., or with the social philosophy of Calvin Coolidge. On the contrary, the economic basis and concrete implementation of the ideas of freedom and democracy have changed enormously and continuously ever since 1776—a perfectly natural and inevitable process. And a quick glance at the statistics of lynchings, for instance, teaches immediately that the enforcement of civil liberties has made headway during the same decades during which the growth of economic regimentation and bureaucracy allegedly undermined our free institutions. That growth of civil liberties, therefore, has at least not been prevented by the economic policies of the period.

Further, modern democracy in its original, western European form had a young capitalist bourgeoisie among its main standard-bearers, but this historical and revolutionary role does not characterize twentieth-century capitalism in Europe. This is no longer the eighteenth-century capitalism of small independent manufacturers and traders, of groups that were anxious, above all, to free themselves from the fetters of feudal bondage, absolutist monarchy, and guild restrictions

---

[1] See, for instance, Cleveland Rodgers, *American Planning* (New York, 1947).

and to secure a cheap and steady supply of free mobile labor. This is the twentieth-century capitalism of big corporations, combines, cartels, tariffs and subsidies, and, last but not least, a literate, active, and well-organized working class.

In America democracy has thus far been taken for granted by an overwhelming majority of all the principal classes; in Europe, however, or in large parts of it, democratic programs and policies today are more often identified with socialist or labor organizations than with any others. At the same time, leading industrialists in Germany, Italy, France, and elsewhere have badly compromised themselves by financial or moral support of totalitarian movements and regimes at home and abroad. To serious students of recent European history, any assertion that capitalism there has been a champion of democracy while socialism has encouraged totalitarianism must sound like an absurd perversion of the facts.

It is true that in countries like Britain or Switzerland democracy is almost universally taken for granted by all major classes and parties. It is also true that a fraction of the working class in some other nations followed the lead of the Communists even at a time when the latter were more candid in their contempt for democracy than they have been in recent years. Yet real mass support for the idea of freedom and the institutions of democracy in countries like France and Germany, Spain and Argentina, Poland and China has come primarily from parties or movements that were also identified with some brand of economic planning or even full-fledged socialism—two concepts that are by no means necessarily identical, as will be shown later.

To realize these facts obviously settles nothing with respect to the economic and social merits of free competition and public planning, or of capitalism and socialism—two sets of poles that, may we repeat, are not necessarily identical. It simply puts the whole debate about social control back on the plane where it really belongs—that of the comparative economic efficiency and social desirability of the various systems in question. It rids the discussion of the fixed idea and absurd premise that we have to suffer misery—periodically at least—in order to be free and that the elimination of recurrent bankruptcy and unemployment is bound to court totalitarian oppression.

The Real Danger to Freedom

History teaches that freedom or democracy as such are compatible with either competition or planning, either capitalism or socialism, depending on the concrete historical pattern, but that none of these economic systems automatically guarantees freedom unless the great majority of the people really believes in freedom, keeps a watchful eye on it, and is willing to fight for it if necessary. This belief and enthusiasm have been seriously affected in other nations by the misery and desperation that resulted from the great depression.

In our day depression tends to breed oppression. There is no greater danger to freedom than the existence of millions of idle, frustrated, low-income workers; of bankrupt farmers and storekeepers; and of disillusioned business leaders full of fears or subconscious guilt complexes. The stake in any major depression in our intricate mechanized economy is higher than ever before: it is freedom itself as well as material welfare and, in the last resort, peace. The example of full mobilization of resources, both human and material, during a brief national effort in wartime, has made us all wonder whether it really takes a Pearl Harbor disaster to put us fully to work and to keep us at it. This is precisely the underlying issue of full-employment programs and, more generally, of social control of economic life in a democracy.

There is, indeed, every reason to be on our guard lest we succumb to that totalitarian pseudo-solution which involves dictatorial types of control and "full employment" for aggressive warfare. Genuine concern about the future of freedom is a healthy sign in a democracy, and it deserves appreciation. It is time, however, to discard the outmoded attitude from a bygone era that considers *any* concerted action of organized society against recurrent misery futile and dangerous.[2] The stakes are too high in our day to permit a relapse into

---

[2] This includes the fatalistic fringe, that is, those who believe that the rhythm of natural and human events inevitably applies to economic life, whether planned or unplanned. See E. R. Dewey and E. F. Dakin, *Cycles: The Science of Prediction* (New York, 1947).

a philosophy of complacent inertia toward economic disturbances that may again threaten both freedom and peace. There must be a way to wipe out in the world all of those modern plagues—unemployment and thought police, depression and oppression.

CHAPTER II

The Laissez-Faire Solution

LAISSEZ FAIRE as a policy has been dead for decades, if indeed it has ever existed in any strict sense. Laissez faire as an idea, however, has remained fairly strong, even though its general aims have been increasingly out of tune with the economic practice both of private business and of governments.

The gist of the laissez-faire idea, may we recall, is the belief in a constant automatic adjustment between supply and demand, consumption and investment, wages and employment—in short, among all the determining factors of economic life. The price is assumed to act as the main tool of progress and, indirectly, as a virtual guarantor of a pre-established social harmony. The laissez-faire economics of the early nineteenth century, in particular, implied that no serious disturbances could occur (or persist) under such an automatism.

Today some die-hards of that philosophy still maintain that whatever disturbances have occurred were due to the absence of true laissez faire rather than to its existence. Even England and the United States during the forties and fifties of the nineteenth century were, in their opinion, not sufficiently free from government intervention to guarantee an undisturbed play of that automatism. They seriously believe that business cycles, for instance, could be avoided today if only government bureaucrats could be prevented from tinkering with the delicate mechanism of competitive enterprise.

Support for the extreme form of laissez-faire economics has been dwindling, both among economists and businessmen. To begin with, modern research on the causes and phases of business cycles has shown that cycles would probably exist under pure competition no less than they do under our partly regulated competition today. The severe consequences of business fluctuations since the latter part of the nineteenth century have encouraged public intervention, perhaps more than any other factor. Moreover, few businessmen and fewer social scientists in our period are prepared to accept all the social effects of an undiluted laissez-faire policy, such as slums or soil erosion.

Business Cycles and Freedom

If business cycles, with periodic slumps and mass unemployment, are granted to be an inevitable consequence of a competitive economy—whether it is of the chemically pure or the partly regulated type—then there is only one other line of defense for contemporary supporters of laissez faire, and it is precisely this line behind which many of them are taking their positions today.

They admit freely that business fluctuations, including periodic slumps, are an unavoidable effect of a competitive system; but they hasten to add that this is the inescapable price of freedom. Mankind, they state, cannot eat the cake and have it any more than an individual can. A nation that cherishes its liberties and, therefore, wants to avoid a constant and growing regimentation has to pay the price. If any particular individual gets under the wheels and, in a depression, joins the army of bankrupt farmers or unemployed workers, well, that's just too bad for him; it would be far worse for him and his fellow citizens to live and work under a dictatorship.

This attitude is exposed to criticism from at least two directions. First of all, it overlooks the growing intensity of economic disturbances and the extreme difficulty in our period of getting out of a slump once it has occurred. There is no need here to dwell upon the fact that our industrial economy has grown far more rigid than was the economy of the nineteenth century. We may choose, it is true, to disregard those types of rigidity that have been due to government intervention, such as tariffs and subsidies, although in most of these cases the government intervened under the pressure of the private business groups concerned. We may even choose to assume that all the existing government regulations would be removed as soon as we decided to follow the advice of our laissez-faire advocates, although no practical pattern for such complete removal has yet been submitted. We may finally assume, just for the purpose of this discussion, that labor as a social group would switch over to a laissez-faire philosophy to the extent of cutting out any union interference with the free play of wages.

Even under these most unrealistic assumptions enough factors of economic rigidity would be left to impede drastically the market automatism on which we are expected to rely in overcoming business slumps. The volume of capital frozen in an industrial machine of growing intricacy, the concentration of economic power in a relatively small number of big corporate concerns, the cost of effective advertising and salesmanship, and many other factors have made an impressive but somewhat clumsy colossus out of our industrial economy. Even if government and the unions, through some sort of miracle, should overnight disappear from the economic scene, a depression of the length and intensity of that after 1929 might occur and persist at any time.

The Lesson of Economic Mobilization

Moreover, the assertion that such disturbances, with all the individual sacrifices they involve, are just the inevitable price of freedom has no real evidence to present in its favor. On the contrary, there is every reason to believe that either periodic slumps or constant misery, in addition to being socially unbearable, are also economically superfluous today. Detailed calculations make it appear likely that, for the first time in the history of mankind, the world could be technologically equipped within a measurable space of time to produce, under peacetime conditions, enough food and other essentials for its entire population. It has likewise been discovered, especially under the impact of the war emergency, how quickly we can step up our production and keep it at a high level and how thoroughly we can lick extensive unemployment within a year or two. This success has been achieved at the expense of a very considerable growth of the national debt; but even if the direst predictions of orthodox economists concerning the ultimate effect should come true, which is very doubtful indeed, the result would hardly be more devastating than another depression on the scale of 1929–1932, not to mention a greater one.

For the time being, at any rate, most of us are impressed by the ease with which we managed to cope with the needs of total warfare and yet to lift our standard of living well above the prewar level. In the midst of the war effort, per-capita purchases of consumer goods and services in the United States, valued at prewar prices, went up from $508 in 1939 to $589 in 1944, an increase of 16 per cent.[1] Private business cannot very

---

[1] *The Impact of the War on Civilian Consumption in the United States, the United Kingdom and Canada,* Report of a Special Combined

well claim exclusive credit for such achievements, since these results were achieved under far-reaching government planning or regulation. To the extent that private enterprise actually accounted for our production miracle in the Second World War, we should try to learn from the type of economic framework that enabled it to achieve during the war what it had been unable to do equally well before.

At the same time, few people will seriously assert that we had less political or intellectual freedom under the wartime type of economic control than we had before. In the midst of a total war we freely elected and criticized our President and Congress, and we discussed constantly and in full freedom everything under the sun that was not a military secret in a rather specific sense. Our mild wartime censorship was abolished long before the War Production Board or War Labor Board. Our wartime record of civilian liberties was, if anything, better than it had been for earlier periods. Even under the adverse and exceptional conditions of a war for survival, a broad program of economic control or regulation turned out to be quite compatible with political democracy and intellectual freedom.

During the war we also improved our statistical techniques in evaluating consumption needs, production possibilities, materials and labor available, and many other data that are equally valuable in foreseeing and

Committee set up by the Combined Production and Resources Board (Washington, 1945), p. 21.

influencing the trend of business activities in peacetime. Do we really have to scrap permanently this newly
acquired knowledge and technique just because some of
our fellow citizens are constantly haunted by the bogy
of a dictatorship from excessive foresight and alert-
ness?

"The State" and We

They are quite unaware of the fact that they are
anarchists at root. The whole idea that "The State" is
necessarily the deadly foe of the individual and that
you can only be free if organized government confines
itself to the duties of a nightguard (or if it preferably dis-
appears from the social scene altogether) is in the tradition of nineteenth-century anarchism in its more primi-
tive forms. It is completely out of tune with the basic
philosophy of democracy—a philosophy that assumes
that a government that is freely elected and controlled
by the majority of the people can generally be relied
upon as their helpful servant, even though its actual pro-
gressiveness and efficiency will always depend on the political maturity of the citizens themselves. "Liberty,"
says Ralph Barton Perry, "is morally justified when its
exercise is consistent with, or conducive to, the excercise
of other liberties; or when it resists encroachment by
other liberties which fail to take account of it, and make
room for it. . . . The extent to which a man may be
considered a lover of liberty is then to be measured in

terms of his passion for the liberty of others." [2] It is strange to observe the frequent confusion of liberty and license when economic interests of an individual or a group are at stake.

Clearly the semianarchistic misreading of democratic principles can in part be explained by certain traits of early American history. The initial experience of a nation in the making, vigorously striving to shake off the rule of a distant and unimaginative government, has left its imprint upon social concepts in America up to this date. These concepts, of course, were also influenced in their formative period by the general revolution of the young bourgeoisie in the western world against the shackles of feudal society and an absolutist State.

During the colonial period and the early years of the American Republic, "The State" was identified by many with a leviathan, or at least with the incarnation of foreign oppression, social reaction, arbitrary taxation, and a centralistic bureaucracy. For over a decade after the Declaration of Independence some of the former thirteen colonies struggled desperately against the establishment of a powerful central authority. Fortunately the wisdom of the Founding Fathers that led them to establish safeguards against the abuse of political power, also overcame all resistance against an ade-

---

[2] *Puritanism and Democracy* (New York, 1944), pp. 518, 520, quoted by permission of the publisher, the Vanguard Press.

quate Federal authority; but the mistrust of government in general and of a strong Federal government in particular persisted long after any danger of renewed foreign oppression had passed (and long after anarchism, as a conscious political doctrine, had almost completely disappeared in the western world).

Perhaps that basic conflict is best expressed by comparing a statement by George Washington with one by Henry David Thoreau. The first President, in his Farewell Address, said:

Remember, especially, that, for the efficient management of your common interests, in a country so extensive as ours, a government of as much vigor as is consistent with the perfect security of liberty is indispensable. Liberty itself will find in such a government, with powers properly distributed and adjusted, its surest guardian.

But Thoreau, a child of the nineteenth century, started his essay on "Civil Disobedience" with the words:

I heartily accept the motto—"That government is best which governs least"; and I should like to see it acted up to more rapidly and systematically. Carried out, it finally amounts to this, which I also believe,—"That government is best which governs not at all"; and when men are prepared for it, that will be the kind of government which they will have. Government is at best but an expedient; but most governments are usually, and all governments are sometimes, inexpedient.

Let us come back, however, to the economic solutions which the contemporary rear guard of laissez faire has to offer as an alternative to purposeful government action against either periodic or steady misery. Fundamentally, this rear guard still believes that a really free competition would automatically take care of these and other evils. Its members are rightly concerned, however, at the actual barriers to free competition, which have developed historically through the growth of monopolistic combination and through concentration of economic power in general.

They are not opposed to government intervention to the same extent that the early nineteenth-century generation was. While they share its belief that governments should keep out of direct business activities, they have virtually abandoned hope that the business community itself will establish and maintain real freedom of competition if it is only left alone. They assign to the government the essential task of enforcing continuously certain specific rules of the competitive game and, in particular, of preventing the formation of market monopolies.

The Outlook for Trust Busting

Ever since the Sherman Act of 1890, trust busting has been a rather popular if sporadic activity of the United States Congress and Government. In recent years Thurman W. Arnold, Senator O'Mahoney, and, with a different approach, Henry A. Wallace have been among the leading advocates of that type of government intervention designed to keep down the dangers to free competition from private business itself. It is important to realize that this whole concept of "planning for competition" is distinctly American. In Europe, including Great Britain, it has long been assumed almost generally that the trend toward monopolies, for right or wrong, has come to stay; and government intervention or outright socialization has often been advocated on these grounds. The question arises whether any basic difference in economic trends between European and American capitalism can explain this divergence in economic philosophy, which affects both supporters and critics of that system in general.

Some of our trust busters think of monopolistic restraints in terms of a sinister conspiracy through which wicked criminals try to undermine the established practice of competition, somewhat on the lines of bootlegging gangs or illicit trade in narcotics. In some cases, indeed, such restraints actually have all the marks of a conspiracy, but this is merely incidental to the far broader issue involved. Others conceive of competition as a kind of continuous sporting practice or game like, say, chess. The competing partners play primarily for the fun of it; and after the smarter one has won, the government, in a combined role of attendant and referee, hastens to restore the original position and to have the game start all over again.

Actually, business competition is a very peculiar sort of game, and the stakes involved are very high indeed—for the audience and referee just as much as for the players themselves. Some people overlook the fact that competition, from the businessman's point of view, very seldom represents a self-purpose in the sense of a mere device to kill time in an interesting way. What he is usually interested in are profit and influence. After a fairly moderate level of money income is achieved, his purpose, subconsciously at least, is no longer just making money in order to live more comfortably. He is increasingly dominated by a drive for power or, more specifically, by the urge to prove to others and to himself just how smart he is. In this particular sense competition, as the potential road to profit and power, could be compared to a game.[3]

But here the comparison ends. In business life the successful player tries to keep for good the figures or trumps won, and he will use them against the next opponent if he can. Moreover, the rules of the game are relatively vague and subject to change as new types of industries, business forms, and markets appear on the scene. And the personal stake in this game is life or death in terms of wealth and income and of social position—and sometimes even in a literal sense, if, for instance, we think of Ivar Kreuger, the Match King. If a fighting drive or competitive self-assertion has to be satisfied in our period, as it did in the past, it would certainly be safer to channel it into sports, into card

---

[3] This comparison is actually developed into a full-fledged mathematical system in the *Theory of Games and Economic Behavior*, by John Von Neumann and Oskar Morgenstern (Princeton, 1945).

games, or, best of all, into a rivalry for the greatest contribution to social welfare.

Generally speaking, a crowding out of weaker competitors and a restrictive combination designed to control the market both result from the desire to maximize profit and, thereby, personal power—the same desire that, in the last analysis, underlies ordinary, generally approved business. As long as there is private business for profit, it will inevitably endeavor, as a rule, to outsmart and possibly to drive out all real competitors; or, where this is impracticable, to join up with them in order to maximize profit (and, in a depressed condition of business, to prevent mutually ruinous underselling). In other words, the constant drive toward monopoly in our period is a direct and, in a sense, logical outgrowth of competition, rather than a sinister conspiracy against it.

All this has not been said in order to defend business monopolies or to minimize the antitrust activities of the government. On the contrary, trust busting has been of great value in uncovering business abuses, especially artificial restrictions of supply at the expense of the consumer. In its general economic purpose, however, it has been waging an uphill fight, and after more than half a century of antitrust activity the picture is a rather frustrating one.

Small business, it is true, has physically survived in great numbers, and the terrific mortality every year has been made up or exceeded by the constant flow of new-

comers. Much, however, of the *relative* economic share
it had in the past has been lost. Concentration of economic power has made rather constant headway and
the Second World War, with its sudden need for efficient mass production of war materials, has accentu-
ated this trend.[4]

To the extent that trust busting attempts to turn
back the wheel of history, it is bound to be hopeless.
The actual choice today is not between the small-
business forms of our forefathers and the monopolistic
combinations of recent years, but between the latter
and social control of economic life. At the same time,
the case for such control does not rest entirely upon
the historical self-destruction of competitive enterprise
alone. Nor, for that matter, does it depend on a belief
in the "maturity" of our industrial economy, which, in
the absence of compensatory activities of the State, is
supposed to lead to a secular stagnation. Without going
into the merits of any such argument, it should be clear
that the intrinsic laws and limitations of competition
itself, under present-day conditions, construct a sufficient case for social control of economic life. This question will be discussed later in greater detail.

---

[4] See *Economic Concentration and World War II*, United States Senate, Special Committee to Study and Survey Problems of Small Business
Enterprises (Washington, 1946).

Laissez Faire Today?

The laissez-faire solution, both in its original and in its modern forms, has overlooked these practical impediments to an effective automatism of national markets, not to mention the gigantic obstacles to a really free competition in the international scene such as tariffs and quotas, basic differences in the standards and habits of living, and the growing economic impact of war preparedness. At the same time this whole philosophy has persisted in claiming exclusive rights to individual freedom for an economy of periodic chaos. In one critic's words, "I yield to no one in the importance I attach to free enterprise and individual development. But this conviction of the validity of individualism and individual development as the supreme goal of community organization, the end towards which all government and economic activity must be directed, cannot be identified with any particular economic system or type of government." [5]

Business disturbances could not be expected to disappear even if real laissez faire should be re-established today—a utopian assumption indeed. At the same time, the social dislocation wrought by any major depression in our day is such that no nation can afford to rely upon an eventual readjustment through the market mechanism, if for no other reason, then because of the serious

---

[5] J. B. Condliffe, in *Proceedings of the Institute of Economics and Finance,* Occidental College, Los Angeles, 1945, p. 158.

dangers to freedom and peace that such social dislocation is likely to entail.

Why, under these conditions, a great many people—
businessmen and others—hesitate to draw the right
lessons from the interwar experience remains an interesting question for the social psychologist. The reproach
of "idealism," which faces any alternative offered to the
competitive automatism, has a very peculiar sound if
compared with the "realism" of the disaster generation
of 1929. We come fairly close to the truth if we allow
for the influence of profit hopes for the future, even in
lines that may be bankrupt at the moment or outmoded
permanently; for individual or group drives for power,
regardless of the social interests affected; for the tenacity
of vested interests; and for plain inertia. It is uncertain
at the moment whether or not the scattered support
from British business circles, in coal mining for instance, for the Labour government's control program
marks the beginning of a new attitude toward economic
goals.[6]

Some of the alternatives to laissez faire that have been
proposed or actually employed during our lifetime have,
indeed, been of a dubious or plainly disastrous character. This applies, above all, to totalitarian solutions.
A laissez-faire policy today is utopian; a totalitarian
policy is devastating.

---

[6] See the address by Sir Clive Baillieu, President of the Federation of
British Industries, as reported in *Labour and Industry in Britain*, Feb.,
1946, p. 25; also the speech of his successor as president, Sir Frederick
Bain, before the American Chamber of Commerce in London, *New
York Times*, Dec. 17, 1947.

CHAPTER III

The Totalitarian Solution

THE ROOTS and forms of totalitarianism have been many. They have varied considerably in countries of different social backgrounds. Only an ignoramus can assert that Soviet Communism and German Nazism, for instance, are identical in their historical roots or social significance. It is entirely possible to be opposed to all types of totalitarianism and yet to distinguish clearly between their various causes and manifestations.

To begin with, Nazism is permanently opposed to any concept of democracy, as a matter of principle; Communism professes to be democratic, at least in accordance with its own interpretation of democracy and in the long run. Nazism is always nationalistic in an aggressive sense; Communism is internationally minded, always in theory and at times in practice. Nazism is basically anti-intellectual; Communism is pro-intellectual within the Marxist-Leninist framework. Even if due allowance is made for semantic differences and if some of the distinctions are recognized to be relative, any number of fundamental differences in the social roots of and social forces behind the two systems remain.

The Social Roots of Soviet Communism

The historical bases of Soviet Communism were: first, the rise of a small but concentrated industry, largely controlled by foreign interests, in the midst of a backward peasant country with an absolutist regime; second, the revolutionary impetus and leadership of a limited urban proletariat—or its Marxist vanguard— facing a vast amorphous mass of illiterate peasants; third, the defeat of Tsarist Russia in the First World War and the resulting disintegration of her military and administrative machine; and, fourth, the ultimate necessity for the Soviet regime to do without a world revolution and to foster domestic industrialization in order to secure both a bearable standard of living and an adequate industrial basis for its national defense.

The Soviet type of totalitarianism had originally arisen from the minority position of the working class —and in particular of the Communist Party—in a backward rural society. It had continued in the form of a suppression, by the Stalinist wing of the party, of those who stuck to the concept of world revolution. And it continued once more when a course of fast industrialization, at the expense of an early outlook for adequate consumers' supplies, was adopted after 1927. Around the middle of the thirties there were certain indications of greater freedom of thought, but the increasing danger to peace and eventually the war itself soon put an end to any such trend.

This rapid survey is not meant to deny the existence, in specific spheres of life, of some freedom of expression in the Soviet Union. This applies, for instance, to managerial affairs of a plant, as long as the Communist philosophy, party, and institutions are taken for granted as the general basis of discussion. Neither is it meant to imply that the Soviet Union is necessarily on its way toward western forms of free expression and that it has merely been delayed temporarily in this development by the impact of the war. Last but not least, we must not overlook the legacy of oriental mistrust and despotism, which was taken over from Tsarism and which, thirty years after the revolution, still hovers over Russia.

What matters for this discussion above all is the absence of any comparable roots of totalitarianism in the western world and, especially, in the English-speaking countries. There is no recent heritage of feudalism or absolutism; there is no backward peasant class that would far exceed in numbers the industrial workers; there is no dominating influence of foreign interests upon industry; and there has been no military defeat that would have shaken the traditional structure of government and society.

Instead there is a century-old tradition of free opinion

and of individual initiative in a broad sense—not necessarily that of a business firm only. Mass organizations
of labor in these countries were originally of the trade-
unionist type only. The existence of long-range political
objectives in the labor movement has been of fairly
recent date in Great Britain; it is still controversial in
the United States, even when such objectives remain
based on the general assumption of a continuing capitalist society.

In short, such roots of social control of economic life
as may exist in the West, especially in the United States,
are completely different in nature from those of Soviet
planning since the revolution of 1917. Soviet planning
succeeded the semifeudal economy of a Tsarist State
rather than a basically competitive economy; and the
Soviet dictatorship followed the Ochrana, the secret
police of Tsarist Russia, rather than any freedom of
opinion. Whatever may be the shortcomings of the
Soviet system from the viewpoint of western individualism, it certainly is closer to western concepts of social
and racial equality than was Tsarism; and it has elimi-
nated the political rule of an unimaginative reactionary
absolutism, which before 1917 had been thriving on a
perennial condition of widespread illiteracy.

The recent movement toward social control in the
western countries has been of an entirely different origin, which we have already discussed; it has been a
reaction to the imperfect functioning and social evils
of an uncontrolled competition such as had never

existed in Russia at all. The isolated success of proletarian revolution in an extremely backward and largely precapitalist society in eastern Europe, instead of in western nations with "ripe" industry and capitalist concentration, was surprising from the viewpoint of Marxian thought itself. This point will be discussed later.

The Social Roots of Fascism

The Fascist type of totalitarianism has been of a quite different origin. True, it has shared with the Soviet State such techniques of domination as the one-party system and the secret police, but this outward resemblance should not be allowed to obscure the fundamental social differences between them. Especially is this true of that most radical attempt at Fascist totalitarianism, German National Socialism.

While Fascism has constituted an international danger ever since the early twenties, it has appeared in nationally different forms in each country stricken by it. Precisely this national adaptation has been part of its strength. At a time when the attempts of the Comintern at international equalization and imitation among workers' parties failed miserably, the International of the nationalists functioned splendidly in the Spanish Civil War and on other occasions. Not only the color of their shirts but the psychology and concrete aims of their propaganda varied significantly from country to country in line with the traditional prejudices and habits of thinking, and also with the social and political structure

34

of each nation. To speak of Fascism in a general way, therefore, would involve an attempt to bring Nazism and Shintoism, Mussolini and Perón, Franco and the Ku Klux Klan under one formula. Such an attempt would have limited value. Even if we confine our attention to those major countries where some brand of Fascism has been in actual control over a prolonged period, generalization still remains difficult.

Moreover, the Japanese brand of Fascism, in its historical and religious roots, has been too different from any western movement to allow fruitful comparison. The semifeudal structure of Japanese society, which survived right into the period of industrial mechanization, the peculiar impact of an Oriental religion in its adaptation to imperialist expansion, the insular position and natural poverty of the country, and the absence of any democratic background or experience, just as in the case of Russia—all discourage any attempt to draw either positive or negative conclusions for western trends from Japan's road to totalitarianism.

The case of Argentina is not clear enough, at the time of writing, to permit any generalizations. The Perón regime, to be sure, shares with European Fascism its totalitarian ambitions, its militarist nationalism, and its demagogic mass appeal to the underdog; but it has risen to power during a period of war-born prosperity, apparently without clean-cut support from the big economic interests. Possibly its social pattern is closer to that of nineteenth-century Bonapartism than to that of twentieth-century Fascism, but we shall try to avoid the strait jacket of rigid classifications. It is certain, at any rate, that the sad lag of social security behind present-day needs gave Perón one of his most effective weapons of propaganda, especially among the under-privileged rural masses.

This leaves Italy and Germany, the former as the first major victim of the Fascist virus and the latter as the nation that developed the most vicious and aggressive brand of it. Both countries had been very late in their national unification; both of them had undergone disappointment and humiliation in the wake of the First World War, an experience that further contributed to a kind of national inferiority complex with its nationalist overcompensation. Both countries were highly industrialized in some sectors and yet had retained big rural estates of feudal origin, which gave continued influence in politics and society to a class of reactionary landowners. In both countries small business and the peasants were either crowded out of their properties or, more frequently, were reduced to misery and economic insignificance by the concentration of business power in industrial combines and bank concerns. In both countries periodic depressions and mass unemployment had helped arouse, at different times, a socialist antagonism toward the capitalist system in an organized and active working class, along with a vague reactionary anticapitalism in the middle classes. In both countries an influential group of business leaders felt that strong governmental action against the economic evils was indispensable, but they preferred to keep organized labor on the outside and to have the job done by groups they could trust, without any interference by others.

Both in Italy and in Germany a solution of the evils mentioned appeared to many as possible only in the form of additional *Lebensraum* to be acquired at the expense of other nations. Such a course presupposed a far-reaching adjustment of the whole economy to future aggression, based on ruthless elimination of any possible opposition to war preparations. These were the main roots of Fascist totalitarianism in Italy after 1922 and in Germany after 1933, if we disregard the failure of Hitler's first attempt in 1923.

Boom and Bust in Germany

In order to understand more clearly how a highly industrialized nation with old cultural traditions and some democratic experience could succumb to totalitarianism, it is worth while to recall briefly what happened in the Reich during the crucial years before 1933; for it is a very shallow philosophy that tries to explain totalitarianism in Germany, or any concrete behavior of nations in our period, entirely from immutable national characteristics, either bad or good, rather than from changing social structure and institutions.

The "rationalization" boom of 1927–1928, which had been fostered by foreign loans, had speeded up the concentration of economic power in the hands of great industrial combines. An elaborate structure of tariffs and subsidies encouraged the formation of cartels, but the German economy as a whole remained of the capitalist, private-enterprise type. At the same time, labor unions of both the socialist and the Catholic types also gained ground, and their political outlets, the Social-Democratic and "Center" Parties, were the mainstay of the Weimar Constitution and the Reich Government when the world crisis of 1929 struck.

Its impact upon Germany was devastating. One reason for this was the speed of industrial expansion during the preceding years, which had been accompanied by a vast increase in labor-saving methods of work. Other reasons were the sudden stop in the flow of foreign credits, the indirect effect of a collapse of banking concerns on an industry that was still partly dominated by them, and a deflationary fiscal policy, especially under the Brüning government—a policy which was understandable (which does not mean excusable) in a country that had experienced, less than a decade before, an unprecedented runaway inflation due in part to unbalanced budgets.

Whatever had been the ultimate causes of the slump, its effects upon the middle-class and labor population were disastrous. Several millions of workers were thrown out of their jobs. Those most frequently affected were the young ones, who had only recently left school and had not had time enough to acquire skill, experience, and seniority. Some of them joined the ranks of the Communists, but many more succumbed to the lure of shiny uniforms and relative security, which the Nazi Stormtroops offered. Another large group fluctuated uneasily between various types of extremism, uniting in one conviction despite their bloody skirmishes in everyday politics: the conviction that they could not rely upon the slow and ineffective methods of German democracy—the only kind of democracy they knew—in coping with the emergency from which they suffered so badly.

They were supported in this belief by thousands of small handicraftsmen and storekeepers, whose business methods dated back to medieval times. These groups blamed both major classes of industrial society—capital and labor alike—for their misery. Similar attitudes prevailed among millions of peasants and farm laborers, who had been hit by an agricultural slump long before the general crisis of 1929, and who suffered from a debt burden that was unbearable in a period of low prices.

All of these groups were angry with one another and with nearly everybody else. All of them were looking for scapegoats and panaceas. They blamed for their sufferings the politicians, the labor unions, the profiteers, the Jews, the foreigners, the reparations, and above all "The System," meaning the supposedly slow, inefficient, and corrupt ways of democracy.

Freedom began to lose whatever meaning it had

acquired for them during the preceding years. Freedom no longer meant free speech or worship. Increasingly they associated it with a mere freedom to starve and to be an outcast of society; freedom to be disunited and weak in a situation that called for purposeful prompt action.[1] They cried for a strong man, without looking very much at his program or real aims—a dictator who would offer a new and vigorous approach to the national emergency and would set an early end to their misery and frustration. *Any* kind of purposeful action seemed to be better than mere reliance on automatic recovery at some uncertain date.

Perhaps all this makes little sense to a western reader, who not only knows the ultimate outcome of that experiment, but who has been brought up in a tradition of freedom much older and firmer than any that ever existed in Germany. Perhaps he will recall that a similar economic emergency had very different effects in the United States, for instance, in the same crucial month of March, 1933. And yet he may retain an uneasy feeling. Regardless of the disturbing factors mentioned in the earlier national history of Germany, that mass madness actually broke loose there during one of the peri-

---

[1] The *New York Times Magazine* of Aug. 11, 1946, printed on page 26 a letter from a veteran, which contained the following passage: "The power of the government to take decisive action in any domestic problem has been nullified in the general rush back to freedom from Government interference. We veterans gave up our freedom, too, and now that we have it back, it doesn't look so good."

odic depressions from which the whole capitalist world had been suffering, in varying degrees, for well over a century. Those unemployed workers, peasants in debt, and backward craftsmen were undoubtedly "wrong," especially in the light of their more recent experiences, when they backed a Fascist totalitarianism after the economic disaster of 1929; but who could argue sensibly with misery and frustration? Who could guarantee that they would not have similar effects elsewhere next time?

We should not forget, however, that additional and decisive support that the assassins of freedom in Germany received during the years of depression—the support from the upper classes, including top leaders of private business as well as aristocratic landowners and military men. The latter's quest for unlimited control of governmental policy and finance, designed to tide them over the slump; their desperate reliance upon rearmament as the only possible source of a boom that would lead them out of the deadend alley of a depression "multiplier"; and, above all, their vague but uncomfortable feeling of responsibility toward the impoverished workers and middle classes for a disastrous slump that their economic leadership had at least not prevented—all these factors resulted in an ardent desire on the part of the upper classes to support a movement which promised to shift the responsibility to very convenient scapegoats: the depressed and impoverished

41

groups themselves, as represented by their traditional organizations and "The System," plus the Jews and foreign nations.

The details of this upper-class support have been too often discussed to need itemizing here. It is sufficient to recall the financing of the Nazi Party and its Stormtroops, especially during the critical days of their bankruptcy in 1932, by the great industrial combines in the West and the Junkers in the East; the earmarking for the Nazis of part of the subsidies that the industrialists and the Junkers alike had received from the government, directly or indirectly, at the expense of the average taxpayer or consumer; the Harzburg agreement of October, 1931, and the subsequent alliance, sealed at the home of Baron Kurt von Schroeder, a leading Cologne banker, on January 4, 1933, among representatives of big business, the aristocratic landowners, and the Nazi Party; and the eventual coalition of these groups, symbolized by Hugenberg, Papen, and Hitler, in the first government after the downfall of the Weimar Republic.

The Rearmament Cure

The point is that no sinister ambitions of prosocialist planners were at the root of totalitarianism in Germany. It was rather the deadly enemies of the labor and socialist movement there—big business, the Junkers, and the Nazis—who combined in order to form the Third Reich, while both Marxian and Christian Socialists, in different ways, resisted totalitarianism to the bitter end. Their methods were quite ineffective, to be sure, and the price was untold sacrifices by thousands of their members. No semiconscious undermining by reckless planners of the German democracy, which until 1929 was about as sound as democracy had ever been in that part of the world, but rather the local effect of a world-wide depression, one of the periodic business fluctuations of the competitive age, fostered the mass despair and cynicism from which the Nazi demagogues profited. The tolerance and indirect support of Hitlerism by western appeasers should, of course, not be over-looked.

It was, in short, not economic planning but the absence of it, in any sense of maturity and integration, that killed German freedom. Fascist totalitarianism had seized the imagination of the masses because it promised them exactly what the only free society they knew had failed to bring them—security along with prosperity.

The solution that Hitlerism offered was, indeed, fallacious and disastrous. At first, however, the masses did not realize that the cure was even worse than the disease. Unemployment disappeared; business, large and small, gained ground once more; a great flow of public spending stimulated economic activities long before J. M. Keynes' *General Theory of Employment, Interest and Money* made its appearance in the western world and, from a very different angle, shook the conventional concepts of financial policy there. It took the Germans, and quite a few foreign observers, several years to realize fully the two gigantic drawbacks of Nazi prosperity: dictatorship and war.

The pattern of Nazi dictatorship would have been bad even if it had not aimed at eventual aggression. Its recipes against depression included the smashing of labor unions, with jail or death for independent labor leaders; the elimination, therefore, of all free bargaining between labor and management and the end of any union influence upon wages and labor conditions; the regimentation of manpower distribution; the compulsory organization of agriculture in the *Reichsnährstand*, with checks upon the free disposition of peasant landholdings; regimentation of the individual business unit; and draconic sanctions, with the ultimate threat of the concentration camp or death penalty, for the violation of such government codes as price control. Of course, the spending policy of the Nazi government, based on an expansion of monetary circulation and combined with an increase in open and concealed taxation, also had an important share in the business revival.

Yet the effect of these Nazi policies might have been short-lived if they had not taken an early turn toward rearmament and aggression. The drive toward the creation of a great armed force helped the average German overcome his feelings of individual frustration and national inferiority. Its interaction with reckless nationalist propaganda produced, temporarily at least, a national effort and a spirit of sacrifice without which neither Reichsbank spending nor the Gestapo terror could have been fully effective.

Somewhat later Germany's great fishing expedition into the resources of other nations got under way. The first beachhead was established through subsidized dumping of German industrial articles on foreign markets, while unusually attractive prices were offered for the primary products of these nations. It was followed up by an ever more ingenious network of barter, clearings, and debts, and by splitting up the Reich currency into dozens of separate categories. Eventually, outright blackmail and military invasion were applied when the trade relations between the countries concerned and Germany had become hopelessly entangled and confused. In other words, the whole pattern of Nazi planning would have been inconceivable without a pre-established purpose of exploiting other nations and milking them in every possible way, including eventual conquest and looting of their resources.

Why this totalitarian solution for the evils of the depression collapsed ultimately is too well known to require detailing here. Hitler's widely advertised intuition failed him at the decisive point, and blunders of a military and psychological nature alike prevented Germany from exploiting her initial successes in the Second World War. The indomitable resistance first of Great Britain and then of the Soviet Union gave the United

States the necessary breathing spell to throw the weight of her industrial power into the scale, especially as totalitarian Japan had similarly failed to exploit her initial success at Pearl Harbor. The margin of victory was fairly narrow, to be sure, and the danger to the victims of aggression was very great from 1940 to 1942.

The outcome of totalitarianism for Germany has been disastrous indeed. She has emerged from her adventure in a state of far-reaching physical devastation, economic and political disruption, and greatly reduced manpower, territory, and resources. The Nazi solution for the depression evils, from which the whole adventure started, turned out to be immeasurably worse than either the evils themselves or the more old-fashioned cures of the laissez-faire type. Germany is out as an aggressor nation and as a great power for a long time to come. So are Japan and Italy. Are we certain, however, that some other nation may not seek its refuge from another wave of depression and unemployment in a totalitarian pseudo-solution?

Between Scylla and Charybdis

What conclusions for the economic policy of the future and, in particular, for the fight against business disturbances and unemployment should be drawn from the failure, in quite different ways, of both solutions discussed? Can a new approach to the problem of individual freedom and social control be worked out in such a way as to avoid the pitfalls and frustrations of laissez faire and totalitarianism alike?

Misery and oppression are both about as old as mankind, but their modern forms are interrelated in a peculiar way that differs from older patterns in some important respects. No longer is misery in the western world due primarily to the uncontrollable whims of natural forces, and no longer is oppression explained mainly by the absence of any tangible concept of freedom. Misery in a world of gigantic productive resources and oppression in a world that has known concrete forms of freedom both result in our day from surrender or default on the part of a generation that has every technical facility to know better and to do better.

There is no greater enemy of freedom today than mass insecurity. There is no greater enemy of peace today than mass insecurity. Prolonged unemployment engenders misery and frustration, which in turn lead only too easily to the cry for a strong hand, for prompt action of *some* kind, for an end to parliamentary slowness, and for scapegoats at home and abroad—in other words the cry for a Führer, for a cure at the expense of other nations, and, finally, for expansion and war. Insecurity today tends to destroy freedom; loss of freedom tends to foster war. The fantastic logic of our perverted world is convincing once you accept its absurd premise, that is, once you accept the dogma that nothing can be done about the basic causes of social insecurity without endangering freedom and peace!

47

And you do accept this dogma, implicitly at least, as long as you believe in an economic automatism that promptly heals every wound if only it is left alone; as long as you rely on the "natural" laws of the market, the same laws that for over a century have led to periodic depressions of increasing gravity in the capitalist sector of the world; as long as you endow the individual businessman with the same myth of infallibility that the authoritarians attribute to their dictator; as long as you uncritically assume the harmony of individual drives for profit or influence with social goals of prosperity and security; as long as your economic philosophy recognizes sacred cows of any kind.

This is certainly not meant to encourage an attitude of social passivism or nihilism. On the contrary, the ultimate purpose of the independent judgment recommended is to foster well-considered action. The worst enemy of bold effective measures in the real interest of society is the complacent reliance of the man in the street upon supposedly infallible men or groups, regardless of whether they are dictators, business groups, or labor organizations.

The fundamental role of organized labor in any social reconstruction today will be discussed later, but it should be said at this point that an attitude of "labor cannot be wrong" is of just as little help in solving the economic issues mentioned as are other types of prejudice. If organized labor, along with other groups, confines itself to a day-to-day fight for better income and occupational conditions within each industry—certainly commendable aims in themselves—then it is bound to run periodically into the same difficulties that beset business along with every other group in our economic society. Organized labor will have to emphasize and initiate broad planning for prosperity and security on a national and international scale in order to stop cyclical slumps with the concomitant unemployment, financial strain, and mass despair.

What is necessary today, above all, is clarity, candor, and courage to speak out on basic social issues. So far supporters of such economic reforms as a full-employment policy have, as a rule, found it necessary to justify their ideas in terms of fostering free enterprise, usually without any exact definition of this concept. Henry A. Wallace, in his book *Sixty Million Jobs*, advocates "democratic planning to preserve our free-enterprise system" (p. 32), while he criticizes a Planned Economy, with capital letters, as a threat to freedom. He identifies it with "the absolute planned social-economic life of the regimented state," as opposed to the type of national employment budget he suggests as an example of democratic planning. Similarly the United States Senators who wrote the draft of the Full-Employment bill of 1945 justified it by saying, "It is the responsibility of the Federal Government to foster free competitive private enterprise and the investment of private capital." Even so the concept of full employment and the bill itself were not found acceptable by the majority, which eventually passed a very diluted and reduced version of the bill called Employment Act of 1946.

In its original meaning the term "free enterprise" referred to the laissez-faire concept of business activities, that is, a market free from governmental regulation of interference in accordance with the economic philosophy of the early nineteenth century. This is obviously not what the authors mentioned a moment ago have in mind, for they have incurred the wrath of tradition-bound economists, politicians, and businessmen precisely by advocating a rather far-reaching governmental intervention in the shape of a public guarantee of an adequate level of employment. What these authors really mean by "free enterprise" appears to be, first, room for individual initiative of everyone, whether businessman or not; and second, the existence, not of "free" enterprise in the sense of a state-free economy, but of privately owned or managed enterprise—a very important difference indeed, as will be shown later.

Huey Long, the would-be dictator of Louisiana, who was as sharp-tongued as he was reckless, once said that if there were ever going to be Fascism in the United States, it would be called "anti-Fascism." That was a cynical remark, but one might suspect that if there ever is social control of economic life in the United States, whatever its type it will be called "free enterprise." Apparently the human mind, or that of our contemporaries at least, is set up in such a way that it feels safer in calling new institutions by an old name. Or perhaps the process of intellectual realization and linguistic adjustment has been outdistanced in our day by that of social change. We need not worry too much about this lag, yet there is a distinct danger in failing to realize fully the range of adjustments that are either necessary or under way already, or in confusing the real issues at stake. If we find it indispensable to carry out significant alterations in our economic mechanism because it has not functioned as well as our grandfathers thought it would, why not say so with courage and confidence?

Most of us, fortunately, have not hesitated to criticize and turn down the totalitarian pseudo-solution for such evils of our period as depression and unemployment. It is all to the good that the downfall of the Axis has opened the eyes of many with respect to the fatal character of the Fascist cure for those evils. What we still need is equal clarity concerning the deceptive character of laissez-faire slogans from a bygone era. We must have a clean-cut elaboration of the type of economic planning compatible with the political and cultural freedoms dear to all of us—in other words, the type of socially controlled economy that will help to eliminate the periods of economic chaos that are a deadly threat to our freedoms.

CHAPTER IV

Freedom and Order in Economic Society

HOW can we meet the need for social control of our complex, intricate economy and yet preserve and expand the benefits of individual initiative, which modern society needs at least as badly as did earlier periods? How can a drive toward constant progress, which can only originate in freedom, be channeled and guided by organized society in such a way that it does *only* good?

Before this issue is discussed specifically, clear understanding is needed of certain concepts that are often distorted or confused in everyday debates. To what extent would an economic society of the type mentioned represent either free enterprise or socialism?

The Concept of Free Enterprise

The term "free enterprise," as has been indicated already, has become one of those convenient catchwords that sometimes help establish a sham unity of national purpose where no genuine unity exists. Free enterprise has been a slogan for conservatives and liberals, for social reformers and old-fashioned reactionaries, for corporation presidents and union leaders, for small storekeepers and monopolistic combines, for farmers and professors, for government officials and, at one time at least, for the Communist Party of the United States. Certain writers or statesmen who profess ardent support for freedom of enterprise are at the same time dubbed collectivists by their critics. It is sufficient to mention again the name of Henry A. Wallace. What is behind this Babylonian confusion and how can we get the discussion of economic policies out of this maze of semantics?

Obviously the term "free enterprise" has been used by the various groups mentioned in different and often contradictory ways. When the National Association of Manufacturers uses this term, then it really means private property, either large or small, with as little interference from the government as possible. But when liberal reformers use the same term, then they are likely to mean individual initiative in a broad sense without reference to any specific structure of property. In other words, the term "free enterprise" in the former case refers to ownership privileges that are actually enjoyed today by specific individuals or economic groups; in the latter case, however, it refers to an unimpeded development of ideas and activities—especially those aiming at improvements—by every individual, regardless of whether he is a self-employed businessman, a salaried manager, a farmer, or just a plain wage earner. Finally, the term "free enterprise" is also used sometimes in the specific sense of an absence of legal or actual obstacles to the establishment of *new* business units, especially small stores or shops.

Free enterprise in the exclusive sense of an uninhibited development, within a well-defined framework, of individual initiative and resourcefulness should be an element of the economic society of the future to the same extent as in the past—and possibly more so. In fact, one of the main reasons for the recent drive toward economic reform has been the growth of impediments to individual initiative as a result of depressions, unemployment, poverty, insecurity, and, especially, of monopolistic restrictions. On the other hand, free enterprise in that other sense of the unqualified preservation of the property structure and group privileges that exist today could not be reconciled with the requirements of an effective control of economic life by organized society. It is high time that the artificial fog in which the whole concept of free enterprise has traditionally been shrouded be dispersed. Everyone who uses this concept should make clear exactly what he means, instead of taking a basic agreement for granted and thus creating the illusion of a unity that is not borne out by the facts.

Changing Meanings of Socialism

A comparable confusion has been prevailing in some quarters concerning the concept of socialism, especially in its relationship to free enterprise and, more significantly, to freedom in general. To begin with, the term "socialism" has often been subject to misleading use by the identification of one specific form of socialism (or of movements seemingly related to it) with the whole thing. Thus, when Mr. Jones speaks of socialism, he refers to the anti-Soviet, humanitarian, pacifist, and at times isolationist "progressivism" of Norman Thomas. But when Mr. Smith discusses socialism, he means the Five-Year Plan and, perhaps, the one-party system in the Soviet Union. After all, the Soviet Union's official title is Union of Soviet *Socialist* Republics, and its official terminology conceives of "socialism" as a temporary, imperfect phase of a development that will eventually lead to communism.

When Mr. White refers to socialism, he means Hitler's Nazism, which included the word Socialism in the title of its party, with the full consent of the big-business groups that financed it, in order to steal the thunder of the original socialist movement that was its deadly enemy. But when Mr. Black speaks of socialism, he means precisely this original movement as represented by the "pink" Social-Democratic parties and trade unions in Europe.

Finally, the term "socialism" is sometimes used in

the United States in order to classify a New Dealish
movement toward moderate economic reforms, the
same movement that likes to classify itself as a champion of "free enterprise." To complete the confusion,
rightist and pro-Fascist elements in every country long
ago dropped any practical distinction between socialism, communism, and contemporary liberalism. They
identify any supporter of economic progress or change
with totalitarianism on Soviet lines and include a number of ardent spokesmen for free enterprise (though
not in their own sense) in their classification of communists. Basically, of course, they simply need a Red
Bogy in order to present themselves as the saviors of
society, just as Hitler did with good success at home
and abroad for quite a while.

We do not intend to add to this confusion, which has
not always been unintentional, by coining new defini-
tions and trying to make them exclusively valid. What
really matters is that everyone who uses such concepts
today—and who does not?—should both know himself
and make clear to others just what he means. "Socialism" in the sense of a Fascist totalitarianism is most
certainly incompatible with the kind of individual freedom that we have recognized as an indispensable
feature of a desirable economic society. Nor is the Soviet
concept of freedom—namely, social freedom from
private exploitation without any effective safeguards for
positive rights of the individual—applicable to the ways

and needs of western societies. On the other hand, the socialist movement in Europe, particularly in Great Britain, has always emphasized the importance of individual rights and initiative. In some parts of the Continent it is actually the only vigorous representative of such ideas.

Socialism in the general sense of an effective control over economic life by organized democratic society has lost much of its horror to western nations in recent years. However, the desirable scope of collective property (as compared with other methods of social control, such as legal regulation, mixed enterprise, or the mere setting of a specific framework for business activities) remains a subject of controversy, and the exact answer is bound to vary from country to country. Many Americans have come to accept a far greater responsibility of democratic society for the proper functioning of economic life than they used to. At the same time, organized socialism in Great Britain, for instance, has come to believe in a variety of control methods, compared with its earlier concentration on changes in property titles alone.

Herbert Morrison, one of its chief spokesmen, has defined its underlying philosophy today as follows:

Britain is the first great nation to attempt to combine large-scale economic and social planning with a full measure of individual rights and liberties.[1]

---

[1] *Labour and Industry in Britain*, Dec., 1946, p. 181.

Nationalisation, socialisation, public ownership, are not ends in themselves, and the Socialist who imagines that is all that he has got to think about would not need to have a big brain to think about that. . . . As I have said, socialisation is not an end in itself. The object is to make possible the organisation of a more efficient industry, rendering more public service, and because of its efficiency and increased productivity enabled to do progressively better for its workers.[2]

There will be, and in a sense ought to be, a good deal of business activity carried on among us without State operation or control [but it will not be allowed to become] a breeding ground for economic insecurity and periodic depression which has been our curse in the past. The State must possess and act upon a moving blueprint of the community's productive organisation. Where it does not operate it or control it, it must at least understand it and the factors that work it. By this means it can use its own power to regulate where it does not own or operate.[3]

Other British spokesmen have worked out various devices designed to decentralize as much as possible the actual administration of controls. This has included schemes for autonomous control boards of a semipermanent type, which would make the daily practice of control and planning independent from mere whims of the voters and their representatives, while reserving for them the ultimate right of long-range decision. Others, however, believe that whimsical wrecking of controls will be kept down by the conservatism of citizens toward

---

[2] *Official Report* 418, Hansard 969, Jan. 30, 1946.
[3] Herbert Morrison and associates, *Can Planning Be Democratic?* (London, 1944), p. 21.

institutions of policies which have actually gotten under way, especially if a democratic delegation of power has successfully been carried out. Occasionally the Tennessee Valley Authority has been mentioned as an example of decentralized social control in the Western Hemisphere.

More generally, there has been an increasing realization of the difficulties implicit in any *general* nationalization, with public management, in a large country with diversified industries and an intricate economy such as Great Britain. Even in the incomparably smaller setting of New Zealand, frequent warnings against the dangers of centralization have been issued, for example in various writings of Horace Belshaw. On the whole, however, the pattern of New Zealand planning has been designed chiefly to reduce the vulnerability of the economy through indirect devices such as guaranteed prices for dairy farmers, subsidies for other primary producers, and an elaborate system of social security. Despite a substantial amount of governmental landholdings, New Zealand represents an untheoretical attempt toward socio-economic planning without much nationalization, rather than an experiment in Marxian socialism.

This brings us to the relationship between the concepts of socialism, planning, and social control, which have certain elements in common but are by no means identical. One statement by F. A. Hayek with which we agree is that "it is possible to have much planning with little socialism or little planning and much socialism." [4] In particular, a more specific discussion is required in order to define the actual significance of the various methods of social control and the way in which they can best be combined with individual initiative.

Types of Economic Planning

Can a general economic plan allow leeway for individual initiative? The answer depends inevitably on the type of plan one has in mind. It has lately become a fashion to picture economic planning in general as a supercentralized dictate of one man or an omnipotent clique at the top. The rest of the government machine and, indeed, of the whole nation concerned is supposed to take orders blindly, without questioning them or adding any suggestions of their own. As a theoretical construction, it is not impossible to imagine such a type of planning, but it is pretty hard to believe that any sane person could advocate it for a complex industrial society.

In fact, even the concrete types of totalitarian planning in our period do not quite conform to that bogy. In the Nazi economy private ownership of plants and stores prevailed, and much depended in each of them on individual decisions of the owner or operator. The Soviet manager and the organized workers' groups in his plant have a considerable amount of discretion both in helping shape that part of the general production

---

[4] *Collectivist Economic Planning* (London, 1935), p. 15.

plan that concerns them and in carrying it out in detailed practice.

Granting, however, that the totalitarian type of economic centralization, even within its actual limits, is quite incompatible with western ideas of individual initiative, there is still no reason at all why the specific, historical pattern of planning in either Nazi Germany or the Soviet Union should be considered the only conceivable ones.

Let us recall those kinds of economic activities, within both the national and the individual spheres, that today involve decisions comparable to those that are implicit in economic planning. How does a government—including those of nations with a relatively close approximation to free competition—prepare its annual budget? It first collects information and advance estimates from its various departments, which have in turn collected them beforehand from their subdivisions and field offices. The final budget may not give each of these departments and offices all it wants, but it will give most of them an opportunity to administer in detail the funds appropriated, to make certain adjustments as the necessity arises, and to suggest improvements for the future.

In appropriating a certain amount of money for national defense, for instance, Congress—acting in this case as the head agency for fiscal planning—does not attempt to tell the War Department experts which type of radar they should order. It leaves these decisions to the individual initiative of the officials in charge, though it may ultimately hold them responsible for an efficient use of the funds appropriated. Virtually the same principle applies to the state government or municipality in its schemes for highway construction or garbage disposal, and to any good-sized corporation in its planning for the year or two ahead for each of its factories or stores. It even applies, in a sense, to any family in which father earns the money but leaves the detailed administration of the household budget to mother's private initiative.

In other words, planning at the top, with delegation of executive power in matters of detailed administration, is a general principle that inevitably permeates wide spheres of any complex society, though the degree and forms of such delegation may vary greatly. What would distinguish a socially controlled economy from the present state of affairs in North America would be, above all, an extension of such planning from the spheres mentioned to those of production and distribution more generally, and an integration of scattered schemes already existing in various fields of national activity.

It has often been pointed out that private enterprise, too, is inevitably engaged in a kind of planning. Much of it, indeed, is "competitive planning," that is, planning how to outsmart a number of other competitors, rather than how to integrate the activities of the company with those of the economy as a whole. However, the latter element must also be represented in the schemes of any company that is hoping to do effective business. In the words of Bishop Bromley Oxnam as reported by the *New York Times* of June 13, 1946, "The American Telephone and Telegraph Company plans. The Ford Motor Company plans. The railroads have realized the same necessity and plan for tomorrow. Are we to believe planning is wise everywhere except in the commonwealth itself?"

Even within the field of public planning there are striking inconsistencies in popular attitudes. While national planning still meets much mistrust and opposition, city planning by now is pretty much taken for granted. The difference is not merely in geographical scope. City planning, by and large, concentrates on *physical* readjustments, even though some changes in property relations are often involved in zoning or traffic regulations, for instance. National planning, it is true, is sometimes interpreted in America in a similar way, that is, as physical co-ordination of public works or soil conservation; but it means more often—and in this discussion—the organized, rational handling of social problems that are known to exist or are expected to arise.

This means that a purely formal conception of planning would be meaningless. No such thing as planning for *indeterminate* ends, whether of a material or a cultural type, could really be imagined. Planning is inevitably guided by social goals of a specific character and consists fundamentally of a conscious choice of priorities by public agencies in the interest of these goals. This, we hasten to add, need by no means involve any curtailment of freedoms, except perhaps the "freedom" to live in filth, to breed epidemics, or to lynch. Aside from such elementary self-protection, which no society —whether planned or not—can entirely dispense with, it will be up to the majority to define or redefine periodically the concrete social goals for which general planning is to be carried out. These goals will be in the spotlight of free public discussion all the time. Once they have been adopted by the majority, however, they will guide planning for the period concerned.

What would a general economic plan look like concretely? It would start out from a comprehensive picture of the resources available for use, such as manpower, minerals, energy, industrial plant, and farm land. It would then compare these resources with the patterns of national consumption, which are known from experience. It would give these patterns every consideration in defining a national consumption scheme of socially desirable character, which might, for example, provide for improved housing facilities. It would next compare this general aim with the purchasing power available to the various groups of consumers, and with their known habits of spending and saving. It would finally attempt to arrange both the use of the resources available and the distribution of national income among the major social groups in such a way that it all "comes out" on an adequate level of supply and consumption. There is no reason why such a procedure should necessitate any consumer rationing or allocation. If, as we assume, the national consumption scheme follows closely the long-range pattern of consumer preferences, which is known from experience; if the production scheme is flexible and designed to serve the consumer; and if this policy is integrated with broad facilities for consumer education on a voluntary basis, then compulsion on the consumer level can be avoided.

All this may sound like a terrific task in practice, and in many ways it is. Actually, however, much of the work described has for some time been done, or at least prepared, in the United States and elsewhere. Great progress has been made, both before and during the war, in securing statistical data on such factors as the national income, specific patterns of consumption, and the industrial resources of the nation. What really remains is the integration of our economic knowledge and, above all, its practical application to the economic process. The United States is in a better position to do this than most other nations insofar as it has statistical techniques of greater exactness at its disposal and as it has been spared physical destruction from war operations.

The technical essentials of economic planning in general, which have been mentioned, have of course been discussed in far greater detail by various authors such as Barbara Wootton. What really matters today, however, is a clean-cut choice among various possible *types* of planning—a choice that has a decisive bearing upon the condition of freedom that has here been assumed as indispensable. There is an endless variety of possible types, but in the last analysis they all boil down to the following major groups:

(1) *The Fascist Type* plans for aggressive warfare. Its initial characteristics include various types of monopolistic cartels or pools in both agriculture and industry, with the full participation of and direction by the representatives of big business. They also include a drive for "full employment" through expanded circulation of credit, public orders, and some degree of compulsory labor following the wrecking of the free trade-unions. In its second phase, which in Germany came very quickly, such planning takes a decisive turn toward the preparation of aggressive warfare. It directs national production, foreign trade, consumption patterns, and every other type of economic activity toward this aim long before military hostilities begin.

Even then regulation of private firms or business groups remains the prevailing method of control. It is carried out by a government in which top-ranking business leaders—of the right shade politically and racially of course—exert great influence. Private ownership and profit remain the rule, although the individual businessman finds himself greatly restricted in the concrete use of his property and in the reinvestment or consumption of his profits.

66

It goes without saying that any application to western countries of this type of planning should be ruled out. *All* its underlying principles are unacceptable to us: its suppression of all civil liberties; its elimination of the free organization of labor or of any other group of society; and the concentration of its economic and other policies upon aggression and total war long before actual military operations start. We can learn nothing from this type of planning, except what not to do. At the same time, it is just as nonsensical to identify planning under Fascism with planning in general as it would be, for example, to identify private property and profit under Fascism with the same institutions in general.

(2) *The Soviet Type* stands for public ownership of all means of production. Such public ownership is all-embracing, if we disregard the private ownership of a negligible amount of tools and livestock designed to serve immediate family needs. The public monopoly of productive property serves as the basis for a far-reaching centralization of both the planning machinery and the political administration. The Communist Party with its subsidiaries represents a minority elite, which monopolizes all forms of political expression. At the same time, it supervises the execution of the economic plan in its details, with severe sanctions for any lack of individual co-operation.

Of course, the plan itself is not taken out of thin air. It is derived, in a very large degree, from both past experience and the current estimates and requirements of the individual production unit, that is, the factory or farm co-operative. It gives the plant manager and his workers considerable leeway for initiative and efficiency, and it gives the consumer far-reaching freedom of choice among the commodities available. Rationing is confined to emergency periods, just as in the western countries.

Yet the Soviet pattern of planning will hardly be found acceptable in any of these countries. The reasons for such rejection are numerous. Above all, private property in its modern forms is more deeply rooted as an institution and is more widely distributed in western nations than it has ever been in Russia. The little investor may be of minor significance today as a business factor, but he remains an influential person in American or French society and politics. The small storekeeper, craftsman, or farmer in the West clings to his little world with far greater tenacity than he did in the Russia of 1917. Individualism as a personal philosophy of life is firmly entrenched. The average little fellow will co-operate and develop ingenious efficiency if he has the feeling of being his own master; but he will balk and sabotage any plan that makes him feel he is "being told," or that seems to destroy his little castle.

This applies to the average worker no less than to the farmer or trader. No economic plan that depends on tangible compulsion, especially on the dictatorship of a monopolistic party, or that leaves no room at all for individual business incentives is likely to materialize in the western world. Any realistic planning there must utilize rather than abolish the individualism and property instincts of the little fellow, and it must preserve all basic freedoms of the individual. That is why the Soviet type of planning can only serve as an important object of studies but certainly not as a model for planning in western countries.

(3) *Interventionism* in a way is the opposite of planning rather than a type of it. It is included in this discussion mainly because it has so frequently been confused with planning by friend and foe alike. Interventionism means a sequence of unrelated, or unintegrated, measures in the economic field on the part of a government—isolated measures designed to improve, at one time or another, the condition of the cotton growers, the sugar refineries, the watch industry, or almost any economic group. It may aim primarily at the protection of prices and the profit level or of wages and working conditions in the industry concerned. Or it may chiefly be concerned with the supply of sufficient fiscal revenues. It may aim at the conservation of mineral, water, or forest resources. It may try to help a community or area in distress. And, above all, it may attempt to cushion the effects of a cyclical or structural depression that is in the making or has already broken out.

The scope of such intervention has grown almost continuously in all the capitalist nations and in some others. The growing intricacy of our social institutions, along with the increasing impact of depressions, has forced every government to intervene ever more frequently. The preparation and conduct of industrialized warfare has, of course, been of even greater importance.

Some of the economic techniques adopted were restrictive, while others were incentive; some were of a purely domestic character, while others were concerned with international markets; some were of a generally useful nature, while many others served special pressure groups or vested interests. A great many of the individual measures concerned were indispensable or, at least, genuinely useful from the viewpoint of a forward-looking philosophy of society. Yet one of the main traits of interventionism has always been the apologetic attitude with which such expansion of government activities has been carried out. Another of its traits has been lack of co-ordination and advance thought, a lack which often led to contradictions among policies that had individual merits but were mutually incompatible.

To the extent that there ever was any such thing as New Dealism in the sense of a concrete pattern of economic policy, it simply represented a cluster of interventionist measures within a relatively brief period. In its readiness to "do something" about the economic emergency, and in its usually progressive approach, it had considerable value; in its lack of integrated philosophy or plan, however, it differed little from other interventionist policies.

In short, that lame duck called interventionism owed its existence to a society that could no longer do without genuine planning and yet could not make up its mind to establish it; a society that preferred patchwork to reconstruction and that was too inhibited to shut the barn door before the horse was gone. Such piecemeal work may have been inevitable under the conditions described, but this kind of economic policy has been in marked contrast to the very concept of planning, in the sense of integrated thinking ahead with action following suit.

(4) *Framework Planning,* the only kind of which F. A. Hayek, for instance, approves, is designed to remove systematically all obstacles to the free play of competition without allowing any direct business activity on the part of the government. Hayek defines framework planning as "an appropriate legal system, a legal system designed both to preserve competition and to make it operate as beneficially as possible." [5] Some of its supporters admit that free competition, left to itself, often leads to economic control by the strongest competitors and, thereby, to monopoly. They also realize the possibility of a conflict between individual interests and social goals, and the danger of a profit drive's leading to such social evils as slums or illiteracy while encouraging the efficiency of private business in a purely financial sense.

They advocate, therefore, two types of government policy designed to clear away the underbrush that impedes the growth of a truly competitive economy: first,

[5] *The Road to Serfdom* (Chicago, 1944), p. 38.

a modest amount of social legislation and a welfare policy to protect the underdog or at least to prevent him from questioning the benefits of a competitive system; and, second, legislative and administrative checks to any monopolistic concentration of economic power. Generally speaking, the State should set up suitable rules of the game and then see to it that they are observed, but it should carefully avoid any participation in the game itself.

In trying to define specifically the fields and activities that such framework planning would have to include, its supporters often come close to the interventionists without necessarily realizing it. Especially is this true of those who, in their understandable antagonism to monopolistic concentration, recommend that the government should discriminate actively against the big concerns in favor of the little fellow—for example, through taxation benefits and subsidies—thus implicitly imposing sanctions on success and growth.

There is no need here to recommence the discussion of the practical prospects of such policies and of the whole framework idea. What should be clear is the spotty, halfhearted, and inconsistent nature of the compromise that it represents. The conceptual difference is great between such "planning for competition" and what might be called "competition for planning" in the sense of utilizing individual initiative in the detailed execution of the broad objectives of a national plan.

(5) *Regulatory Planning* is closely related to both

interventionism and framework planning. The difference, however, in purpose, though not always realized by the administrators themselves, is fairly important. Strictly speaking, the setting of a framework for competition is not planning at all; nor is interventionism, for that matter. Regulatory planning, on the other hand, recognizes specific social goals to be achieved and attempts to reach them through purposeful action; but it confines such action to the establishment of certain rules for private enterprise, on the assumption that the latter will react psychologically in a predictable way that will lead in the direction of the preconceived social goals. The countercyclical policies of the Swedish Government and, in a different way, those of issuing banks in western countries point in this general direction. To sum up, the calculated use of the self-interest of private enterprise, rather than its extensive replacement by public ownership, is the guiding idea of the regulatory type of planning.

A diluted form of it consists of a purely informative and advisory type of planning. The late National Resources Planning Board, for instance, suggested periodically to Congress, the Administration, local authorities, consumers, and private enterprise certain estimates of needs and certain lines of policy. It had no executive power to enforce its suggestions. This type of planning endeavors to make private enterprise more effective within the existing economic framework, rather than to change the latter in any marked degree. The government is thought of as a kind of economic insurance company. (Conversely, insurance in general represents a kind of planning.)

(6) *Full-Employment Planning* is a specific application of the regulatory approach. The purpose in this case is to build certain safeguards against extensive unemployment into the competitive economy, while leaving the general framework unchallenged. In part under the influence of Lord Keynes, this whole school has abandoned any belief in an automatic equilibrium—on a desirable level—among employment, investment, and consumption, without giving up its basic adherence to the competitive mechanism as such. It simply feels that strong correctives are needed periodically in order to make the mechanism work without too much social friction, and it sees the decisive corrective in compensatory spending on the part of the government whenever the total outlays made by private consumers and investors do not suffice to secure full employment.

Such writers as Michael Polanyi and David McCord Wright feel that the frequent disturbances in a capitalist economy are either the incidental effects of poor monetary management or the natural results of economic growth in the absence of any co-ordinating machinery for investment and consumption. They believe that the same problems of monetary management or dynamic change face a collectivist economy as well.

Others have pointed to the risk of inflation, which

74

is always implicit in full employment, that is, the possibility of overemployment. This risk, which is a real one, indicates the need for an integration of the monetary techniques proposed with broader types of public policy; for example, with an investment control that would cover, in varying degrees, the total volume, the priority distribution, and the location of new industries. On the other hand, such economic methods, if combined with other policies discussed, make direct price control for full employment unnecessary to nearly everybody's mind.

Some of the economists grouped around Alvin H. Hansen assume that compensatory spending is a periodic, recurrent task of the government in our "mature" economy, and that a well-considered program of specific measures is indispensable in order to translate public spending into new jobs. They have tried, therefore, to work out an integrated program or "shelf" of monetary measures, public works, and so forth, to be used in case of need. To that extent their program represents economic planning of a carefully limited type. To be sure, they use it reluctantly and their basic intention is to make competition work, rather than to subject it to radical innovations. While they assume a recurrent necessity of such correctives and try to chart the general course in advance, some of them would hesitate to use any such scheme unless and until a depression is around the corner or actually under way. In short, they no longer rely on the market automatism as orthodox economists used to, but they are by no means prepared to replace it by a new mechanism and would rather confine themselves to having the repair tools ready whenever the old machine seems to get out of order.

(7) *Production-Consumption Planning* potentially shares *some* of its general objectives with Soviet planning, but it suggests quite different methods in order to achieve them. Its starting point is in the needs of the consumer. More specifically, it aims at an adequate standard of living for every social group, not necessarily in an equalitarian spirit but certainly without acquiescence in a condition of misery in any social stratum. It compares these consumption goals with the productive resources available for the period of the plan. It may design an expansion of these resources, as far as necessary and feasible, and may allocate those that are physically too scarce to cover the entire goal of consumption.

In other words, the social goal in this case is a supply deemed adequate for the needs of the major consumer groups, and the basic method employed is the advance determination of the specific use of the resources available. For example, if it is considered necessary to supply new housing for, say, ten million people during the plan period, then a sufficient proportion of the steel, lumber, and other building materials produced will be made available for this purpose.

To this extent the policy discussed has certain points

of contact with Soviet planning. The discernible patterns of such a policy in the western world differ, however, from the Soviet system, first, in the extent of public ownership and centralization and, second, in the determination of the nations concerned to avoid any dictatorial methods of enforcement.

The wartime pattern of American economic policy, especially the priorities system of the War Production Board, provides an interesting approximation in the western world to planning along these general lines. The priorities, based on periodic surveys of raw materials and other resources available, attempted to reserve all scarce articles for the social goal set by Congress and the President, in this case the winning of the war. The production planning under the WPB could not, however, provide any usable pattern for a peacetime policy. First, it was of a short-term character and was destined from the outset to disappear at the end of the war. Second, the one great consumer who had to be given unqualified preference over all the others was Uncle Sam or, more strictly speaking, his armed forces. Third, the WPB controls were on the whole confined to those materials which were both war-essential and *physically* scarce, and the WPB was never supposed to establish any comprehensive planning outside this field. It is true that the wartime production policy of the United States involved the creation of a great amount of new public property. However, the sixteen billion dollars' worth of war plant that the government acquired between 1941

77

and 1944 consisted entirely of newly built factories (that is, not of nationalized units). The bulk of this plant was privately managed and was designed to be sold to private companies after the war to the extent that it was suitable for peacetime uses.

Clearer examples of production-consumption planning are provided in various schemes by such British writers as G. D . H. Cole, Barbara Wootton, and (with substantial qualifications) Sir William Beveridge.[6] It remains to be seen to what extent and how soon the current economic reforms of the Labour government—and, for that matter, those of the French, Scandinavian, and other governments—will lead to any comprehensive planning. At the present time British policy appears to emphasize a nationalization of individual key industries, such as coal mining or public transportation, rather than any integrated economic plan. However, statements by Clement Attlee, Herbert Morrison, and others at the Bournemouth Conference of the Labour Party in June, 1946, and on other occasions indicated definitely that such measures were thought of as leading eventually to a planned economy.

In varying degrees, both the economic spokesmen of the British Labour Party and such neoliberals as Keynes

---

[6] "The problem of maintaining demand on the productive resources of the country so that they are employed productively in meeting human needs arises whether industry itself is controlled by profit-seeking individuals or by public authorities" (William H. Beveridge, *Full Employment in a Free Society* [New York, 1945], p. 37). See also J. M. Keynes' statement in his *General Theory of Employment, Interest and Money* (New York, 1936), p. 378.

and Beveridge have pointed out that the issue of property titles no longer appears quite as decisive as it was assumed to be some decades back. The Labour Party considers it quite compatible with its socialist program to anticipate a survival of private ownership in many industrial fields for any measurable space of time, even though the socialized sector may grow gradually. What matters really, in the opinion of most British reformers today, is social control and its purposeful use. Such social control, they feel, may be exerted under either public or private ownership, depending on the concrete conditions in the industry concerned. Socialization thus becomes *one* control method, to be used discriminately; it no longer represents the focus of social reform. Instead of confiscating the milk cow, the government is left the alternative of letting the owner milk it and then perhaps taxing some of the milk away, after first advising the owner indeed as to how to feed and milk the beast in such a way that the total product may be maximized.

Another British author, Mr. J. E. Meade, suggests the creation of a national investment board with a network of decentralized regional agencies. This board should encourage or require all industries over which the government has any control to plan their capital development for three to five years ahead, subject to alteration. The board would dovetail these plans both with its own investment schemes and with those of important uncontrolled industries. Nationalization would be confined to industries with large capital needs,

79

if no sufficient control over them could be obtained by other means.[7] The emphasis in this concept is on production planning through the medium of investment control. It is true that the author would also like to see established an industrial planning commission for the publicly controlled industries and an economic forecasting commission to inform the private sector of the probable course of prices, consumption, and so forth. The latter commission would resemble somewhat the Council of Economic Advisers to the President of the United States, which, indeed, is not supplemented by any of the other agencies proposed.

(8) *International Economic Planning* differs from all the types discussed so far both in its geographical scope and in the political problems involved. The first seven types all imply national sovereignty as the natural limitation of planning. Of course, it makes all the difference in the world whether the unit concerned is, say, Switzerland with its four million inhabitants or the Soviet Union with its two hundred million people. If the country in question depends in a large degree on economic relations with the outside world, then any type of national planning would have to be complemented by suitable controls of foreign trade. Such controls may or may not take over such traditional policies as tariffs, quotas, subsidies, price differentials and outright dumping, currency devaluation, exchange control, or clearing

[7] J. E. Meade and C. J. Hitch, *An Introduction to Economic Analysis and Policy* (New York, 1938), pp. 54, 204, 265.

agreements. They may or may not use such wartime devices as priorities, licenses, or unilateral purchases in bulk. Generally, however, there is no *intrinsic* reason why economic planning should lead to a restrictive policy on foreign trade any more than the lack of planning has led to it in the past.

It is true that economic planning in New Zealand, for instance, has been greatly hampered by the far-reaching dependence of that country on foreign trade. Such difficulties, however, apply in no lesser degree to a dependent economy without planning, as long as international fluctuations of business continue. No greater boon to world trade could be thought of than the assurance of full employment everywhere. For the rest, neither the experience of New Zealand nor that of other democratic countries bears out the claim that economic planning necessarily encourages a trend toward self-sufficiency. Nor has any real evidence been submitted in support of the view that different national systems of economic society cannot coexist or trade today as they have in the past, or that a pluralism of nonaggressive regimes in the world is impossible.

There is every reason to distinguish carefully between planning and restriction. In particular, there are historical precedents both for a competitive national economy surrounded by a high tariff wall and for a highly regulated economy with extensive foreign trade (as well as vice versa). Neither economic planning nor social control as such preclude a growing co-operation and co-

81

ordination of the national policies concerned. In fact, this appears to be about the only hopeful procedure in our period toward a gradual reduction of national sovereignty as an institution.

Generally speaking, it is quite possible to expand the international division of labor among nationally controlled economies. The worst enemies of international specialization in the past have been depressions and war dangers. Incidentally, the whole issue of regional specialization may have to be restated before long in the light of certain equalizing effects of synthetic processes today and atomic energy tomorrow. However, this problem vastly exceeds the scope of the present study.

A nation that depends on foreign trade in a large degree can potentially administer even a straight government monopoly of foreign trade in a more liberal and less restrictive manner than the one in which the traditional conglomerate of makeshift measures has been administered. Control should not be confused with restriction or with bilateralism. It is true that such devices as the most-favored-nation clause or a free gold standard in the world would no longer be applicable, but how much has been left of them in practice after two world wars and a major world depression? Who seriously expects these policies to be restored on a large scale within any foreseeable future?

At the same time, full employment and a general

gain in economic security would expand enormously the need of each nation for the goods and services of the others and the mutual ability to pay. It is, incidentally, quite possible to think of gold as the future basis of exchange among a multitude of nations with a controlled economy. This is said for the benefit of those who still see in "hard money" the only sound basis for international, and national, business relations. It is another question to what extent a future generation will actually need the device of gold, which fundamentally is of a psychological, rather than of a strictly material, character in an insecure world.

It is conceivable, indeed, that the whole pattern of such control of foreign economic relations will gradually shift, that a full-employment economy will eventually place more emphasis on the control of exports than on that of imports, and that it will ultimately encourage rather than discourage net immigration. National controls will undoubtedly include the movement in either direction of foreign loans and investment in order to complement the domestic policies in this field, but here again nearly every nation has already moved away from past patterns of an uncontrolled flow of capital.

All this means, indeed, that an enormous amount of international co-ordination of national policies will be necessary in order to prevent a repetition of the past working at cross-purposes. In itself this does not mean international economic planning in any strict sense. For the time being no international economic planning—in the sense of production schemes to be designed in advance for a period of several years and then to be enforced through administrative action—exists in practice, and it is bound to remain a mere dream as long as sovereign states with different social systems continue to be the political basis of mankind. Whatever movement there has been toward international economic planning has been confined to a drive for some co-ordination of national planning schemes or, more frequently, of economic policies in general.

We hasten to add that such co-ordination, as far as it goes, is of very great importance for our period. Only too frequently the various nations have attempted to save their own house by setting the neighbor's on fire. Currency manipulations, rising trade barriers, and similar devices have frequently been used in an attempt to stop a depression at home without regard to their effects abroad, the ultimate result being an aggravation of misery everywhere. It is of the utmost importance to co-ordinate the national countercyclical policies on the regional and international levels, and to bolster up such co-ordination by permanent international agencies such as the Economic and Social Council of the United Nations, the International Labor Organization, the Bretton Woods Fund and Bank, the Food and Agriculture Organization, and the International Trade Organization. It should be realized, however, that we continue to live in a world of sovereign nations who jealously watch their prerogatives. In such a world international co-ordination will always remain a poor second compared with national policy decisions, whether or not they belong to any of the planning types discussed earlier.

Perhaps the most immediate and hopeful task in the field of international economic co-ordination is a working agreement concerning the development of backward areas and the share of the more advanced nations in this development. Both the discussions of the last decade or two on how to mobilize the idle resources in the western world and the special problems of war disruption have somewhat obscured the fact that for the bulk of world population the main task still remains a development of *new* resources, especially of industrial production. For their national planning this involves the creation of a social machinery designed to absorb periodic unemployment, to prevent the rise of slums, and generally to cope with the social effects of an industrial civilization. Otherwise new industrialization may make social conditions worse instead of better, or it may simply mean the changeover from one form of misery to another.

As long, however, as the formation of new social capital and the development of new resources, rather than the mere utilization of those already in existence, remains the main task, the whole pattern of national planning in these nations will differ from the economic tasks facing the western countries, though the need for social control in general will be just as great. Most of the backward nations face the problem of relative over-population growing worse under conditions of ineffi-cient agriculture and exhausted soils. *Constant* shortage of modern equipment and skills is their main predica-ment, compared with the *cyclical* failure of developed countries to utilize fully their existing equipment and stagnant population.

Once the industrial development of a backward area gets under way, however, temporary shortages of effi-cient manpower may develop. The importance of a well-considered and well-timed supply of initial equip-ment and skill from more developed areas is evident— a need which has rarely been solved satisfactorily through reliance on private initiative in foreign invest-ment. It is essential that the wealthier nations recognize their coresponsibility in the development of other nations in the world community; just as in New York State, for instance, the City helps regularly to finance the needs of the poorer up-state areas.

Methods of Social Control of Economic Life

What really matters is an effective control of organ-ized society over the economic development, the scope of public ownership being merely an incidental, though very important, issue of method. However, the concept of social control itself requires further clarification.

First of all, social control "over" economic life need not be conceived of as a dictate imposed upon the workers, farmers, traders, and other economic groups by an outside force upon which they have no influence. In a democratically organized society, all major groups (and, in the last analysis, all individuals with active political interest) influence constantly the formation and concrete use of social authority. The government, as the chief executive agency of organized society, thus becomes an active factor of social control, without in the least assuming the role of a dictatorial usurper as long as it is subject to constant criticism and periodic free elections by a mature citizenship. In exerting a broad control over productive, distributive, or financial activities, organized society per se need not be any more dictatorial than it is in setting up traffic signals, in building flood-preventing dams, or in trying to keep epidemics in check. But while the necessity of such technical controls in an intricate society with dense population has long been taken for granted, controls in the economic field have remained an object of controversy.

What should be the concrete purpose of social control in this field? The French and Belgians [8] have in part defined it in their term *économie dirigée*. Actually a great number of scattered, unrelated measures of control have long been in existence everywhere, ranging all the way from regulated farm crops and transportation to issuing-bank policy. The field of industrial production has usually been avoided except in wartime. Missing so far in most western countries has been any

---

[8] For example, Henri de Man, *Réflexions sur l'économie dirigée* (Paris and Brussels, 1932).

conscious integration of such measures in a positive program that would include industrial production. The general purpose of such integration would be to secure, first, an adequate living standard for all population groups in line with twentieth-century goals and possibilities; second, the use and development of natural resources in such a way as to prevent waste and premature exhaustion; and, last, the elimination of major business fluctuations, of the specter of mass unemployment, and of the general feeling of insecurity that has characterized western society in recent decades.

Such social control is not identical with economic planning, though the borderline is not easy to define. The latter term has been used in a variety of conflicting meanings, some of which have been discussed in the preceding pages. They have ranged all the way from a mere local zoning to a complete collectivization of economic life. The concept of social control places the emphasis on both the preventive and the constructive aims of organized society in the economic field rather than on ill-defined techniques of economic policy. It is better suited, therefore, to express the underlying ideas of the measures to be suggested.

As for the concrete methods of such social control, some *combination* of the following approaches, to the extent that they are not mutually exclusive, appears to be best suited to the habits, traditions, and predilections of western nations:

(1) *Industry-wide Regulation of Private Enterprise.*

Such regulation exists already in various fields of business in every western country. In the United States, for instance, it has included the railroad industry, the public utilities, coal mining, cotton farming, and many other activities. There are great variations in degree and form, to be sure. Similarly, Great Britain regulated long before the Second World War her dairy industry, her coal production, and so forth. While these industry-wide schemes, as a rule, were indispensable indeed, they were never part of a preconceived long-range policy and no attempt was made to co-ordinate them. In some cases the measures in question confined themselves to the reduction of specific abuses; in other instances they involved either aids to or restrictions upon production. More often than not they represented emergency help to a stricken trade, and those industries that never caused any particular headache to their governments and parliaments were usually left alone. In other words, if social control of economic life should be based chiefly on industry-wide regulations, then the double job of extending such regulations to many new fields and of co-ordinating this whole network of single-industry rules would remain to be done.

(2) *Indirect Control of Production*, especially through financial policy. Such control may be employed either as an alternative to the infinite variety of regulations required for individual industries or on top of such regulations. The administration may try to influence the volume and pattern of national production

through such policies as the manipulation of discount rates, open-market operations, and other policies of the banks of issue; through regulation of the stock market and of investment practices in general; through tax privileges for certain industries and suitable management of the national debt; and through an appropriate credit policy, with direct investment if necessary, of financial agencies of the government such as the Reconstruction Finance Corporation. Other indirect methods of production control include freight-rate policies, foreign-trade regulations, and so forth. Generally the advantage of such indirect methods is in the opportunity to keep detailed rules down to a minimum and to avoid bureaucratic complications. Their drawback is in the relatively uncertain, or not exactly calculable, effect of general and devious policies upon a variety of highly specialized industries. Such indirect controls, however, may be complemented by some direct regulation on an industry-wide scale.

(3) *Industrial Self-Government.* Instead of either direct or indirect controls "from above," preference may be given to a network of industry-wide regulations based on the initiative of, and administered by, representatives of the industries concerned. The advantage is again in the reduction of bureaucratic or legislative complications. The danger involved is, first, in the possibility of monopolistic abuses and, second, in the possible lack of co-operation among the various self-governing industries. In order to achieve such co-

operation, some kind of central agency, consisting either of representatives of the various industries or of the government, would still be necessary.

In order to avoid a degeneration of industrial self-government into private monopolies, various kinds of safeguards might be tried out. The most important of them would be an extensive, influential, and responsible representation of consumers and the labor force in each industry on its executive board. Even so the danger of a publicly sponsored cartelization should not be overlooked. Earlier programs and experiments in the direction of industrial self-government include the National Recovery Administration and its Codes in the United States during the early thirties and, in a very different and far more collectivistic form, the schemes of the Guild Socialists in Great Britain during the twenties.

(4) *Mixed Enterprise.* In order to control a number of key enterprises, the government may secure capital participation, which would entitle it to an active share in the management. It is difficult to imagine any situation in which a government would find it desirable to be a minority stockholder, except perhaps for the purpose of obtaining current inside information. More frequently such minority participation has been the unintended result of emergency assistance or bankruptcy proceedings. For the purpose of this discussion we can assume that mixed enterprise is to mean, as a rule, a government-controlled majority of voting stocks. We can assume that governmental participation, if it is

designed to serve social control, will involve a significant representation of the government on the managerial board and that any such arrangement will be aimed at only in key enterprises of essential and highly concentrated industries.

In the past the successful examples of mixed enterprise proper have been fairly rare. Ordinarily it tends to be unstable and short-lived, for the business aims of the private sector are bound to differ fundamentally from those of the government. Certainly the management of government-owned plants by private companies in the United States during the Second World War cannot serve as a peacetime pattern, especially as it was intended to be temporary from the outset.

Perhaps the most interesting and successful experiment of a related type—namely, the public control of commercial enterprises—has been the London Passenger Transport Board, which replaced chaos by order in the public transportation of Greater London after 1933. In this case agencies of a local government—one of unusual scope and importance, to be sure—were enabled by national legislation to participate in a key industry and to join forces with private interests in integrating its facilities and services. Similarly, the Port of London Authority, the British Overseas Airways Corporation, the Central Electricity Board, and the British Broadcasting Corporation represented various patterns of public participation in, or control of, commercial enterprises. Such influence upon their financial structures and managerial policies was usually achieved by legislative regulation rather than by the purchase of capital shares in the market. On the whole, these forms of enterprise are likely to remain an occasional device for special fields of business activity rather than a generally applicable policy.

(5) *Co-operative Enterprise.* In this case neither property titles nor management are controlled by the government. They are instead in the hands of a voluntary nonprofit association. Whatever may be the merits of co-operatives in general, they can serve as a method of social control only to the extent that their management acts consistently in line with an integrated national policy. Belief in any *complete* organization of society along co-operative lines has waned, and few are those today who would consider social control of economic life possible through co-operative methods alone. Further, co-operative organization in the sphere of production has proved successful only in farming and some specific industries in the field of consumers' goods; its possibilities in heavy industries are extremely limited.

An example of collectivist co-operative organization in farming that is integrated into a general economic plan is offered by the *kolkhozy* in the Soviet Union. While this particular experiment is certainly not applicable to western conditions, co-operative organization in general has undoubtedly some possibilities as one method of social control in such fields as farming and retail trade with their feeding or processing indus-

93

tries. It can serve this purpose, however, only where such voluntary associations have developed on a substantial scale and where they share with a forward-looking government the same social philosophy and the same desire for democratic control of economic development.

(6) *Nationalization.* This term has been used in widely different and confusing ways. Sometimes it has been employed as a synonym for socialization, a concept that will be discussed in the next section. In other instances the term "nationalization" has been used in the sense of state ownership of individual enterprises, in competition with private companies in the same field. Still others apply the term to monopolistic ownership of a whole industry by the government. Occasionally, however, nationalization has been identified with mere influence or regulation by the government in a privately owned industry. Finally, the same term has also been employed in order to classify the taking over by a national government of facilities that were originally owned either by local governments or by foreign interests. In short, while "nationalization" has sometimes been considered as identical with *nationalisation* in French or *Verstaatlichung* in German, it has meant a very different thing in other cases.

In this discussion the concept of nationalization will be used exclusively in the sense of governmental ownership *and* management of a decisive section of an industry. Obviously a lease to private interests of publicly owned plants leaves little opportunity for social control.

There may be exceptions to this rule in such cases as a government monopsony (that is, the dependence of an industry on one major consumer, the government); but whenever the government is the only buyer, it is likely to be very influential even without holding any property title at all. Leases of publicly owned plants, however, are infrequent under peacetime conditions.

Likewise, ownership with or without management by the government of scattered enterprises of no particular importance, in the midst of a business structure that is otherwise privately controlled, offers little opportunity for social control and is generally rather an unhealthy condition. Direct competition between public and private enterprises is usually a nightmare for both. Private business has rightly felt that such competition could seldom be carried out on equal terms, for privileges in taxation and capitalization or political influence would often favor the public units. With equal justification, the managers of the latter have felt subject to administrative, financial, and moral restraints, and to a kind of political supervision that did not apply to their private competitors. Private enterprise is at its best under conditions of real competition; public enterprise is at its best where it can organize a whole industry or area in an integrated fashion. Neither one is equipped to compete efficiently with the other.

Nationalization, therefore, in this discussion refers to government ownership of a whole industry, or a decisive section of it, in an extensive area, with direct

management by a governmental agency, though not
necessarily by the central government itself. Such
management may be carried out in a bureaucratic way,
that is, with centralization of all responsibility at the
top and fairly rigid rules for the manager on the spot;
or it may give the local manager considerable leeway
and freedom of decision in all those matters which do
not involve any policy making or co-ordination with
other sectors of the national economy. The often-
quoted difference in management methods between the
United States Post Office on the one hand and the Tennessee Valley Authority on the other may serve, within
limits, as an illustration of the two alternatives mentioned.

Clearly, nationalization may lead to greatly different
results, depending on the general philosophy and concrete setup of the administration in charge of it. Nationalization, along with some of the other control methods
we have discussed, has been abused by dictatorial or
aggressive governments for their sinister purposes, but
this fact should not be allowed to obscure the use of
technically similar methods by progressive and peaceful
governments as well. After all, an automobile may be
used either by the Salvation Army or by a hold-up gang,
and no sensible person would blame the activities of the
latter on the aims of the former merely because they
used the same vehicle. The same discrimination should
be applied to vehicles of public policy, like nationalization. In itself it is simply a social technique that can

be used either for progressive or for reactionary purposes. This distinction, indeed, brings us very close to the issue of socialization.

(7) *Socialization.* Here again inconsistent use of the term has caused considerable confusion. Aside from being mixed up with nationalization, there has also been some uncertainty whether the concept of socialization should be confined to a revolutionary process of general expropriation of all means of production, in line with Marxian ideas, or whether that concept should include the collectivization of a single company or industry as well.

In this discussion the concept of socialization will apply to public ownership in a specific sense to be defined in a moment. What is meant here by socialization is *not*, of course, identical with embedding the performance of an individual or group in the context of society, a process that is also referred to as socialization (for example, the socialization of education or of art). Furthermore, in referring more specifically to the economic sense of the term, we shall again exclude from our discussion any scattered collectivization of individual business units, which are to remain in competition with private enterprise. Some early Marxians expected that a general socialization of the whole economy could be achieved with a magic stroke "On the Day After the Social Revolution," to use the title of one of Karl Kautsky's pamphlets. This idea is likewise counted out. It is assumed that the socialization of a multitude of industries in any developed country is bound to involve *economically* a lengthy sequence of highly specialized measures even though the *political* shifts involved may be of a more immediate and spectacular character.

What, however, are the distinctive traits of socialization as compared with nationalization? First of all, the concept of socialization does not necessarily mean ownership by a national government. Socialization may refer to state, county, or municipal ownership, or to the control of industries by public bodies specially created for this purpose. Or it may mean some kind of producers' association on a nonprofit basis, assuming that a whole network of such associations should be established.

More important than that, socialization in this discussion refers generally to that kind of collectivization that emphasizes, first, decentralized administration and, second, active control or at least advisory participation in the management by free representatives of organized consumers, organized labor, and other social groups with legitimate interests in the industry concerned. This clearly distinguishes it from nationalization, which places the main emphasis on administration by representatives of the national government.

Here again a purely technical definition is insufficient, although the features mentioned would at least make it pointless to identify, say, the Fascist type of collectivization with this concept of socialization. The

latter kind of social control presupposes a large degree
of voluntary organization, democratic education, and
active interest on the part of the various social groups
concerned in the managerial efficiency and success of
plants and industries. It is also pertinent to consider
the possibility of a "socialized sector" of varying size in
a national economy that would include other forms of
social control along with socialization in the sense indicated. During a transitional period there might also
be an uncontrolled sector in trades of minor economic
significance.

This brings us to the main issue, namely, which of
the control types discussed, if any, lend themselves to
effective application in the western world? The best
answer, we repeat, is some *combination* of all of them.
The degree and form are bound to differ greatly from
country to country. Any attempt to establish social control of economic life would be seriously prejudiced if
any one particular technique, rather than the general
aim of social control itself, should receive the main emphasis. If, for instance, the collectivization of *all* productive property should be presented in a doctrinaire
fashion as the only worthy goal of social change, then
the practical result might be an indefinite postpone-
ment of any change, through failure to utilize financial
methods of control and other alternatives that modern
economics has worked out.

Precisely because of the far-reaching separation of

99

ownership and control in our period—a problem that will be discussed later—any overrating of legal property relations, as compared with actual control of management, should be avoided. In recent years we have seen examples of social control on a wide scale without any extensive collectivization of property, such as in Sweden, and also examples of an attempted collectivization that failed because it was not integrated with other methods of control, such as in France.

It is true that control measures of almost any type are likely to affect and, as a rule, to reduce the meaning of private property as an institution. Even where no formal expropriation of any kind takes place, investment control, for instance, will affect the traditional right of the owner to use and dispose of his property. Moreover, in the United States an owner might claim, under the Fifth and Fourteenth Amendments, the right to derive a profit, or other forms of unearned revenue, from his property title in order to challenge the constitutionality of social control. Such control undoubtedly affects the yield of property, and since it is more often than not the capitalized yield that determines the property value, it might be argued that any type of control inevitably impinges upon property rights.

Without discussion of the legal aspects of the problem, the answer is that every nation and government has always been engaged in a great number of policies that unavoidably affected the use and value of private property. Taxation, inheritance laws, the issue of money, zoning and building restrictions, police protection, sanitary regulations, and war have always affected profoundly all private property. Outside the conventional sphere of government activity, the constant oscillation of business life has threatened property owners with partial expropriation through bankruptcy at one time and through inflation at another. Moreover, the great majority of the people in industrial nations have enjoyed practically no property rights as far as means of production were concerned. Finally, concrete forms and values of property are conceivable only in terms of the legal provisions of the moment, that is, on the basis of a general state charter. No one saw these historical and social conditions of property more distinctly than John Stuart Mill, especially in Book II of his *Principles of Political Economy*.

In short, social control of economic life is only one phase in the historical process of changing significance of property—a phase that will, indeed, require full expropriation in some fields of economic life, but only a relatively slight degree of functional adjustment in others. And if any existing constitution should actually attempt to freeze an outmoded concept of property, then it should be remembered that constitutions, too, are man-made; that all of them provide a machinery for orderly changes in line with the needs of each period; and that their interpretation by the courts has not always been the same, but has rather followed the spirit of the times.

It is not within the scope of this study to outline in detail a practical combination of control methods on the lines indicated. Any such attempt would be futile without specific reference to the location and time period in question, say, Great Britain during a concrete four-year period beginning early in 1949. Nationalization or compensatory spending, for instance, may have far fewer possibilities in one country at a certain juncture than in another country or at another time. Some general statements, however, can be made concerning a combination of the methods mentioned:

(1) The possibilities of both mixed and co-operative enterprise appear to be rather limited, for reasons that were mentioned earlier. They may be somewhat greater in Britain and the Scandinavian countries than in the United States, for the development of co-operatives, in particular, has been long and successful in western and northern Europe. (2) Industrial self-government has somewhat broader prospects, to the extent that it can be based on industry-wide legislation, active participation of labor and the consumers, and an integration of industry schemes into a national economic policy. (3) Indirect control of all major sectors of national economy, especially through financial policies, will be of great importance everywhere. This may apply particularly to the United States, for this country is far less ready for direct controls than are other nations. (4) Nationalization, with direct centralized management by the government, is likely to be employed selectively,

especially where it involves government competition with surviving private companies in the same field. (5) Socialization, with decentralized management, will vary in scope depending on the degree of concentration of economic power and on the efficiency and general condition of the various industries in the countries concerned. It is likely everywhere to keep away from those industries where small business or personalized service prevails, or where the total contribution to national income is slight. It is likely to affect chiefly a number of key industries that could not be reached effectively through indirect methods.

Social control along these lines would seem to avoid many pitfalls of the problem of "economic calculation" (*Wirtschaftsrechnung*), which kept friends and foes of socialism busy during the twenties and thirties. Using the writings of Ludwig Mises, various economists tried to prove that rational calculation would be impossible in the absence of competitive pricing, especially that of capital goods. Meanwhile Oscar Lange and others have shown that even under conditions of public ownership the decisive functions of price and money can be preserved, and that the choice between capitalism and socialism should be made on different grounds.

There is no need here to go into the details of the calculation problem. To begin with, the arguments of Mises and his school stand and fall with the degree of really effective competition on the national and international scale alike. Furthermore, the narrow identification by that school of "rational" calculation with the drive for individual profit finds even less credit today with either economists or psychologists than it did twenty-five years ago. Finally, that school has always concentrated its criticism on the type of socialism that would involve a nationalization of all means of production. Even if Mises' general argument were more convincing than it is, it would affect very little a pattern of social control using nationalization on a limited scale, as one possible method of control, without by any means eliminating all types of markets or all incentives of individual initiative.

Generally speaking, organized society should concentrate on the control of the commanding heights of its economic structure, rather than attempt to penetrate into every little corner. And it should consider carefully just which method of control appears to be indicated in each case.[9] The concrete decisions will vary greatly from country to country, but in many of them the following key industries will be covered in one way or another: (a) Fuel industries, especially coal mining. This applies particularly to Britain today. (b) Iron and steel industry, especially in those countries where it shows heavy monopolistic concentration or where it has relied excessively on armament orders in the past. (c) Public transportation, particularly the railroads. On

---

[9] A detailed analysis of various methods of control, and of the economic choices and decisions implicit in them, is presented by A. P. Lerner, *The Economics of Control* (New York, 1944).

the European Continent, indeed, many of the railroad networks have been publicly owned for a long time, and many lines were built by the governments themselves. Likewise, shipping and the airways in various countries have been subsidized or controlled by the government. (d) Public utilities, especially the power supply. In this field the share of local government in ownership and output has been important in many countries. The United States has contributed the significant TVA experience. (e) Credit and investment. With the elaboration by Keynes and others of the far-reaching dependence of fluctuations in business and employment upon monetary and fiscal decisions, a strong case has been made for social control in this field. For this type of economic policy, ownership changes are incidental rather than fundamental. There is some danger in English-speaking countries today of overrating the possibilities of financial controls compared with others.

This list, may we repeat, should not be regarded either as exhaustive or as equally applicable to every country at any time. It is rather indicative in a general way of the type of policies implicit in social control of economic life in our day.

Individual Liberties and Initiative

Individual liberties and initiative must be preserved in carrying out social control if the latter is to meet the wishes and traditions and get the co-operation of western nations. The assignment is intricate but promising.

Control at the top is by no means incompatible with considerable leeway for the individual on the level of detailed day-to-day decisions. After all, this is the procedure that every efficient chain of stores has had to adopt. The general rule for social control in a democracy, therefore, includes centralization at the policy-making and supervisory levels, with a maximum margin for individual initiative and responsibility at the levels of detailed implementation of the general rules and of their translation into daily business practice.

Profit or, more generally, material rewards for business efficiency cannot be dispensed with for any foreseeable future. To say this does not mean to deny the importance of nonmonetary incentives, even in an economy that is basically competitive. Today citations of merit, decorations, prestige and power in the community, and personal feelings of achievement and superiority are probably no less attractive, in the aggregate, than are the prospects of earning a few or many more dollars. It is true that this fact is seldom realized or openly admitted. Human nature, even that of a hard-boiled tycoon from Wall Street, is far more complex than earlier schools of economists implied, and the single-tracked profit-mindedness that they assumed has really always been a fiction. Certainly all these qualifications apply even more to any economic society in which competitive attitudes have lost some of their concrete fields of action.

There is no logical or historical reason why the spirit

of enterprise should *always* depend on the material rewards that are expected to result from winning the competitive race. Did the heroes of Corregidor fight to the bitter end, with valor and ingenuity alike, for their fifty dollars a month, or did they do it for higher reasons? Plenty of peacetime examples could be cited. Economic man has always been a sad fiction.

Even if we disregard, for the purpose of this discussion, the actual limits to purely material drives today and tomorrow, the necessity remains to reserve for such drives a certain scope of effectiveness. Here again the concrete terms to be applied could be outlined only in specific terms of the location and time period involved, but certain possibilities of a general character might be mentioned:

(1) To the extent that private business property is preserved—and this will apply to a considerable proportion of the total—the same profit incentives that exist today will continue to be effective. What will have changed in this sector—generally in a favorable way—will be the general conditions of doing business and the concrete outlook for profitable operation. In a deflationary situation, for example, compensatory spending is likely to increase the purchasing power of the consumers in such a way that the business turnover rises and profit prospects improve, whatever may be the general merits of such a policy. On the other hand, possible new taxation resulting from the same government program may affect the profit prospects adversely.

Profit expectation and advance calculation as the general method of doing business, however, will remain unchanged in this sector.

(2) To the extent that nationalization, socialization, or any other type or degree of collectivization takes place and that private employers in managerial positions are replaced by public employes, the latter can be allowed a bonus or share in the final profit or surplus—a share similar to that which corporation executives often enjoy today on top of a fixed salary. If the efficiency achievement of the managers cannot be expressed adequately in terms of a tangible business surplus, then some other yardstick of success, based again on existing practices, can be employed in order to reward them for a performance above the average. If, on the other hand, they fail to achieve the standard set, then they should be fired, just as they are by their board of directors today. Political pulls in public enterprise may sometimes be hard to fight off, but how many private corporations are really free of pulls in their personnel policy?

(3) The revenues of the managers in public enterprises may be based on a monthly or yearly quota of the production or turnover, with premiums on any extra performance that is quantitatively measurable. The same principle of premiums or profit sharing could, of course, be extended to the workers as well. In our traditional economy, profit sharing has not been very popular because it tended to accentuate, rather than to diminish,

the general insecurity of jobs and annual earnings. It may, however, have greater applications in a socially controlled economy than it has had in the past. Certainly the fact of broad social control does not preclude individual or group premiums on efficiency.

(4) In certain countries or enterprise units it may be found preferable to express the achievement expected in terms of a concrete margin between maximum and minimum goals, or through a definition of the margin granted to the manager and his staff, especially if the concrete conditions of their operations cannot be foreseen adequately. Here again rewards in the form of individual or group premiums, price allowances, or bonuses can be paid out. Not only the famous "control figures" in the Soviet Five-Year Plans, but some of the wartime schemes of the War Production Board such as the Controlled Materials Plan were made in the form of tentative estimates, which assumed from the outset a certain amount of variation. In order to be effective, any type of planning, whether it is social or individual, must be set up in a flexible way. A mountain climber who encounters unforeseen factors of terrain or weather will promptly change his route rather than break his neck on the trail he had in mind originally, but he could never hope to reach any peak at all if he had not studied the map and guide first in order to work out a concrete plan for his trip.

To choose another illustration, social control, both on the top level and on that of the individual plant, must operate like a military general staff in the sense of having several alternate plans available, from which the one in line with the actual conditions of the moment will be chosen. This method of alternate plans, incidentally, is the way in which smart corporation management has often operated. There is no intrinsic reason why these variations should not be connected with premiums for individual efficiency to the extent that current adjustment depends on managerial decisions on the local level.

(5) The same decorations, citations, special promotions, and extra leaves that have long been applied to both military and business personnel can be used in an economy that is subject to social control. (I hope that no mature critic will use random comparisons with military experiences as an argument for identifying social control with regimentation on the lines of a garrison state!)

(6) Suggestions from the ranks for technological or managerial improvements have not always been looked upon favorably in the past, either because they seemed to contribute to insecurity and unemployment or because they aroused the antagonism of an established hierarchy in the plant. Since social control of economic life may reduce the room for individual initiative in some respects, regular channels for the evaluation and realization of good suggestions should be established wherever possible, and rewards should be given to those who contribute in this way, regardless of their rank or

function in the business unit. Clearly the number and value of such suggestions will depend in large part on the existence of full freedom of speech and wide educational opportunities both inside and outside the plant.

(7) The co-operation of shop stewards, their training in both vocational and economic affairs, and their relationship to a strong, responsible, and democratically organized union movement will be factors of the utmost importance for the success of social control in general and for the development in industry of individual freedom and initiative in particular. In fact, the education of the rank and file of wage earners to an active interest and co-operation in economic policy is an indispensable condition of efficiency in any modern type of economic society. Social control over an industrial economy, in particular, would be hopeless unless it could count on the understanding and participation of its most numerous group.

If and when, on the other hand, such understanding and participation are available, a number of intricate problems in industrial relations will be resolved without too much trouble. It has often been asserted by opponents of social control that the latter is incompatible with either free unionism or free choice of occupation, since it cannot permit any unpredictable or unforeseen wage demands, strikes, or occupational shifts. The objection is valid as long as the average wage earner and his organization are at odds with the regime and its economic program or else confine themselves to getting whatever the market will bear. The difficulties mentioned will be greatly reduced, however, as union leaders and members come to think and act in terms of broad economic progress and social responsibility, rather than in terms of a mere day-to-day struggle for a slightly larger chunk out of the product of an ill-functioning mechanism.

Such an intellectual readjustment of the labor movement has actually been going on for a time, slowly and with setbacks, and yet unmistakably. Whole-hearted co-operation of the unions in the control program will permit the timing of wage demands with rises in productivity and with fruitful possibilities of monetary expansion. The thing to do about strikes is not to forbid them but to make them unnecessary, both by a periodic review of the wage level and by making the labor organizations a full partner in the process of social control. This applies equally to the problems of labor mobility, vocational guidance, and retraining. To the extent that the active participation of labor organizations can be enlisted, prohibitions and penalties can be dispensed with.

All this requires an educational job that has long been under way in some western countries but has been lagging badly in others. Any type of modern industrial economy, whether it is socially controlled or not, is likely to degenerate into a financial or bureaucratic oligarchy unless a labor movement of the type indicated —that is, strong, responsible, and democratically organized—keeps a constant watch upon individual freedom and initiative alike.

(8) Another group of great importance, though far smaller in numbers, consists of the experts in engineering and business organization (in France often referred to as *les techniciens*). One need not believe in the inevitable coming of James Burnham's "managerial revolution" in order to acknowledge the key position of the expert in an intricate industrial society. Whether its specific organization is strictly competitive or socially controlled, it needs the co-operation of scientists, engineers, production organizers, market specialists, statisticians, and other experts if it is to function efficiently.

Certain authors, like Aldous Huxley, are worried at the dangers to freedom that may arise from the growing centralization of power in the hands of scientists and engineers. These experts, it is said, may be dominated by political bosses, who may abuse the mass appeal of the bigger and better future that is expected to result from scientific progress. Other writers, like Elton Mayo, feel that such progress only aggravates the human problems of an industrial civilization—such as fatigue, monotony, and indifference—regardless of the socioeconomic framework under which this industrial development takes place. The industrial worker, moreover, in whom Marx placed such high hopes as the expected agent of social history, may in a little while no longer be needed by industry, says Mayo, if scientific progress continues at the breath-taking pace of recent years.

One need not underrate the current changes in the social role of science and technology in order to consider these theories at least premature. It is quite true that the potential dangers to freedom from scientific and technological changes in our period are no less serious than the dangers arising from economic insecurity. But this need not mean that the scientists and engineers are destined to rule society rather than vice versa. Society itself demands from its technicians a constant adjustment in training and skills. To be sure, some of the special skills that are today in greatest demand and in the highest-paid groups of income may be found useless in a more mature civilization. Society may decide, for example, not to encourage crooners or pugilists in amassing millions of dollars, and it may also clamp down on high-income specialization in horse-racing or in counseling on stock-market speculation.

Allowing for such possible changes in the evaluation of special skills, however, the need for the services of experts will continue in almost any field of social activities. At this point, indeed, the question arises to just what extent the agencies for social control can utilize the skills of the managers and engineers who have run the economy in the past. The answer has to be qualified: to the extent that private enterprise is continued, the changes mentioned in its social framework (such as a policy of compensatory spending by the government) will affect its expert staff very little. To the extent that collectivization in any form takes place room will still be left for the continued activity of those experts whose skills are applicable to the new economy.

Some others may not be so well off. For example, a chemical engineer will find about the same opportunities on the job no matter who controls the plant where he works, but a high-pressure sales manager for the same company may find that his special skills are no longer considered to be of the same importance as they were before. Incidentally, this happened temporarily to many specialists during wartime readjustment of business; others found their occupational background to be of increased value under war conditions. Conversely, a number of high government officials, especially in the economic field, were mobbed with job offers from private business as soon as they became available. This fact, which has applied to such leading New Dealers as Leon Henderson, shows that government service does not necessarily breed bureaucratic inefficiency as has so often been asserted. Or will anyone seriously claim that stale bureaucrats of long tenure automatically turn into ingenious innovators the moment they have a chance to join the payroll of a profit-guided corporation?

With the important qualifications mentioned a moment ago, general opportunities for the majority of experts are likely to grow under social control as a result of the greater economic stability that it promises. The specialist who is willing and able to adjust himself to the tasks that are implicit in the new economic policy, and to co-operate with it—and I do not mean any ideological *Gleichschaltung* at all, please!—will, as a rule, find the same or an improved field of activities. Two questions remain to be answered: First, should experts be employed purely on grounds of technical skills, even if they disapprove in general of the national aim of social control? And second, should experts, on the same grounds, receive a prominent position in shaping and carrying through such social control, perhaps through some shade of technocracy?

As for the first question, the practical application of some skills, especially those of the engineering type, is sometimes independent of the social philosophy of the person concerned, but in many other cases it is not. For example, while machine-tool designing remains the same in any type of economic organization, the distribution of machine tools may change its rules; in the latter case a great deal of economic understanding, co-operation, and adjustment will be necessary on the part of the individual affected in order to cope with the new requirements. If he cannot mobilize any such qualities, then his past skills may be of little avail to the new economic society.

The second question will be answered by every good democrat with an emphatic No. The social rule or privileged position of any small group, or the legal perpetuation of its actual influence, would be a distinct danger to democracy. Moreover, such a policy might hand over the application of social control to individuals or groups who do not believe in it, or who might abuse it for antisocial aims. For example, if the group of experts scheduled to receive a privileged position should include indiscriminately the technological and financial leaders of monopolistic combines, then the intended co-operation and pooling of company resources might be perverted into a network of private monopolies with official support. The borderline between social co-operation and private monopoly may sometimes be thin, and the decision on which side of that line society is to settle down will often depend on the individuals in charge, their background, and their basic philosophy. Dollar-a-year men or any others who owe their income or, more important, their prime allegiance to a private group, rather than to organized society, are seldom acceptable to a government that is fully aware of its democratic responsibilities.

The selection of leadership for social control of economic life, therefore, should follow the established processes of democracy, reinforced by a number of genuine improvements that have long been under discussion, such as the modernization of parliamentary procedures. The selection of aims and men that are to govern society should remain subject to periodic scrutiny and daily criticism on equal legal terms by the humblest laborer and the most highly skilled expert. The experts, to be sure, will be employed significantly in an advisory and executive capacity by an organized society of any modern type, and in the establishment of economic security and progress much will depend on their wholehearted co-operation. The essential safeguard of political democracy, however, is in a broad social basis for the process of constant selection and re-examination.

CHAPTER V

Political Safeguards of Freedom

MOST of us interpret freedom today, not as a frozen, institutionalized achievement, but as a process of continuous fight against changing enemies and weapons. Many of us realize now that the very concept of freedom has of necessity been subjected to historical changes, both in its philosophical basis and in its practical implementation. The real question, therefore, concerns the extent to which traditional concepts of freedom are applicable to a world that is plagued by economic and emotional insecurity alike, and by the constant threat of depression and war. More specifically it concerns the extent to which the political traditions and institutions of the western world lend themselves to social control of economic life. Will they not be blasted to pieces by the administrative requirements or effects of economic regulation, planning, and other methods of public control?

Let us first consider the second, more concrete question. How much of a safeguard against dictatorial abuse of the enormous power involved can be expected from our accustomed political institutions? In terms of the western democratic tradition, the main safeguards would seem to be of the following types:

Parliamentarism

As long as periodic elections are held in the customary intervals, both on the national and on the local levels, one important guarantee of free expression is preserved. We assume, of course, that the elections take place with full freedom for both the voter and the candidate; that there is no legal or practical restriction upon the formation or functioning of political parties; and that the representative bodies thus elected retain the traditional right of supervising their government including, in particular, the appropriation of its financial resources. In short, we assume, if anything, greater parliamentary liberties than have as yet been established in wide areas of the Eastern and Western Hemispheres alike in the course of century-old struggles.

Is there any intrinsic reason why such parliamentary rights could not be applied to a socially controlled economy? It is hard to see any difficulties other than those generally facing representative bodies in an intricate society like ours. It is true that the continuous growth of agenda has placed an almost unbearable burden upon the shoulders of those parliaments that persist in tackling their new tasks with a legislative machinery from the eighteenth century. It is true also that any attempt to have a parliament keep track of every single detail of administration and government spending (and above all, to have parliamentary committees act as a super-executive) is doomed to failure in our day. It is true finally that parliament and its members, in order to act intelligently and efficiently, need a great deal more expert advice in very many fields than they have had in the past.

All this, however, is just as valid—and in some respects far more so—in the absence of social control over economic life. For whenever the absence of such control results in a heavy slump, or in other economic disturbances, parliaments have to work out in haste a series of makeshift solutions. These often require great effort on their part without, as a rule, providing any real way out. Instead of debating methodically long-range plans for economic development, they try to mend the growing holes in the dam through hasty subsidies, tariffs, or other restrictions in this or that industry, without ever catching up with their task unless and until a cyclical upswing brings relief.

In many respects the elimination or substantial mitigation of business fluctuations is the only real hope for parliamentary efficiency in the twentieth century. In emphasizing this we do not mean to deny the necessity of parliamentary reforms in the majority of democracies. This is especially true of the old democracies, since their parliamentary mechanism is usually an old one, too. What really matters, however, in the interest of parliamentary efficiency, is a more secure society and, above all, a more stable economy.

What then should be the main function of parliament in any type of socially controlled economy? It should have, above all, the prerogative and duty to appoint the head planners and controllers; to define carefully the general framework of their agencies and departments; and to supervise in a broad (legal and policy-making) sense the way in which they carry out their assignments. In other words, parliament should determine the goal, set the general course, select the captain, and check up on whether he is heading along the most favorable route toward the goal set; but it should leave to him the responsibility of running the vessel and of managing the details of its operations from day to day. The voters, in turn, should periodically check up on their representatives. They may oust them at the next election in case they disagree either with the goal set or with the selection and supervision of the control staff by the old parliament.

It is very hard to see why, under such democratic guarantees, it should be inevitable that "the worst get on top," as F. A. Hayek has claimed for any controlled economy. What is there in the social mechanism of an *individualistic* economy to prevent the worst getting on top, in business life or otherwise, except the vigor of public criticism and the ethical principles or fundamental beliefs of the average person? Why should it be any easier for bad elements to get on top in economic agencies of public character, which are under constant scrutiny by the parties and their parliamentary representatives? Here again, the administrative record of the TVA, which has been in the spotlight of public and Congressional attention during every year of its existence, is impressive enough.

Here, indeed, another issue arises. What if the voters periodically vote for a change in the party in power, and in doing so, implicitly, for a change in the control program to be carried out? What if they elect representatives who favor river-valley development one year and then fail to re-elect them after four years (or even after two years in the United States)? What will become of the plans that have meanwhile been adopted and partly carried out? Does not planning for several years ahead, therefore, imply a dictatorship of the planners or, at least, of the parliamentary party that started the whole program until it is completed?

The answer is, first, that if a nation, as represented by its parliament, really shows a whimsical disposition, then the only hope in a democracy to prevent arbitrary changes is in an appeal to the good sense and civic education of the voters. If the majority of them are actually immature enough to decide at first in favor of a certain policy and then to refuse it an actual chance to be carried through, then there is no *technical* device that could help. If after a few years of social control they really prefer to go back to insecurity, then no practical alternative remains; for social control of economic life on a democratic basis is only possible with the approval of the average citizen and, more than that, with his active co-operation. There is little reason to believe, however, that the voters of a politically mature nation would succumb to such unpredictable whims. It is much more likely that they would support, for longer than one electoral period only, an elaborate program that looked sensible to them a short time before.

Second, the political dilemma of such control does not differ essentially from that known to exist in many other fields where long-range parliamentary programs are necessary—for example, the foreign policy of a nation. What if the party in power today commits the country to a lasting alliance with some nation that the party in power tomorrow may be against? What about naval bases, foreign loans, participation in an international organization, and a host of other problems?

Such matters have always been decided by the party in power, even though it could never be certain whether the voters would leave it in power long enough to carry through its program. The way in which this is done is to pin down the opposition to the extent of tolerating the general idea of the program at least and, in some cases, to let the opposition make an active contribution to the initial formulation. An outstanding example of recent date is presented by the active part played by Republican Senator Arthur H. Vandenberg—originally an isolationist—in drafting the charter of the United

Nations and in representing the United States in that organization.

Of course such participation of the opposition pre-supposes a mutual sense of democratic responsibility. More than that, it assumes a certain minimum of agreement on social values and national aims. The character of electoral and parliamentary decisions will differ, therefore, according to whether the political parties represent social and ideological groups or merely competing political machines without any fundamental, permanent program or philosophy. In the latter case, continuity of policy has often been possible despite an electoral landslide, with the consequent changes in personnel. In the former case, the potential consequences of a change in majority and in administration are far more serious, for such a change may indicate a reversal of national goals rather than a mere difference in methods designed to achieve a common goal.

Where the issue at stake represents a clean-cut conflict of social groups or diverging class interests, each definitely represented by one political party or alliance, little collaboration can be expected indeed. It is then up to the voters alone to decide whether or not they want the long-range policy to be continued. However, the areas of agreement, or tolerance, are not necessarily smaller in economic reorganization than they are in foreign policy. After the British Labour Party has completed, by 1950, its policy of nationalizing the coal mines, power and steel plants, and railroads, it would be hard to imagine that a new Tory Government in 1951 could turn the wheel back and resell these industries to private interests. It might, of course, make substantial changes in the detailed pattern of government control, but on the whole the Conservatives have already committed themselves not to undo the nationalization carried out so far.

To sum up, there is no valid reason why parliamentarism in the twofold sense of a periodic free election of people's representatives and of their constant supervision over the general goals and methods of social control could not be continued, and it can be fully counted on as one safeguard of freedom in a controlled economy.

Civil Liberties

The first condition of a working parliamentarism is a satisfactory status of civil liberties in general. More than that, civil liberties, however defined, are generally accepted as one objective criterion of freedom. Both the legal equality of all individuals and their freedom of religion are taken for granted in all democratic countries, but it is the general scope and practical application of the freedom of speech—especially political speech—that really decides.

Can the preservation of this indispensable safeguard of freedom be counted on in a controlled economy? There is no intrinsic reason why it should not be. On the contrary, only under the constant fire of free criticism will social control develop those virtues of superior economic efficiency that are its *raison d'être*. Only under full freedom of speech will it escape bureaucratic degeneration and corruption, which in the recent past has contributed, in varying forms, to the doom both of weak democracies and of totalitarianism in various parts of Europe.

It has been argued that the controlling group, vested with enormous economic powers, will be tempted to suppress criticism. However, the potential power of *every* controlling group and, generally, of every governmental structure, inside and outside the economic sphere, has been growing in the absence of conscious social control, too. This growth has resulted from a more intricate pattern of society and from new technological devices—especially in the armed forces—that are automatically at the disposal of every government in a period of developed industry. Yet the status of civil liberties in countries like the United States and Great Britain is, if anything, more satisfactory today than it was in the era of laissez faire and of weak governments. A government that is strong in the sense of purposeful action, efficiency, and the authority to carry out an integrated program is not a liability but a great asset to democracy; and it has turned out to be compatible with a progressive expansion of civil liberties. Simultaneously with that inevitable broadening of government activities, which has taken place in the United States as elsewhere, considerable progress has been made toward racial equality and unimpeded voting, even though much more remains to be done. In other words, social control of economic life can very well be combined with further growth of civil liberties if the people themselves encourage such progress.

More than that, the greater economic security that is expected to result from social control will remove some of the most vicious dangers to civil liberties. Voting for a certain individual or party because of a promise of patronage and, in particular, of a safe government job in a period of recurrent unemployment (the spoils system); the inability of many common people to pay a poll tax or to meet residence requirements for voting because they have to move around in hunting jobs; poor schools and, worse still, failure to make full use of those theoretically available because families cannot afford to do so; the feelings of social insecurity and frustration on the part of poor whites and other under-privileged groups, which are easily translated into bigotry and racial hatreds—all these and many related factors in an insecure society form a constant threat to civil liberties today. No greater boon to these liberties is conceivable than an awareness on the part of organized society of the current need for economic security, and a vigorous policy in this direction on the local, national, and international levels alike.

However, what about that fundamental liberty in a modern industrial society, the right of labor to organize, which inevitably includes the right to strike? Can any economic plan be carried out amidst constant uncertainty whether the jobs planned will actually be done by the workers and on what terms?

The answer is, first, that the rights of labor must be preserved in any democratic society and that provision must be made in any plan both for contingencies of this kind and for those resulting from floods, earthquakes, and other incalculable factors of disturbance. Second, no democratic planning or social control of any kind will work unless labor in particular and all social groups in general educate themselves—as they have partly done in a number of countries already—to realize their responsibilities toward the nation and the world. With increasing maturity and with growing identification of their group interests with those of the new society, the arbitrary and unnecessary type of strikes will probably be kept down to a practical minimum without any repressive legislation. Third, in a general atmosphere of economic security both the material and the emotional causes of labor disputes are likely to decrease. The attitude of organized labor toward social controls and agencies in which it has an active share is likely to differ increasingly from that prevailing toward a strictly private management today.

Democratic Education

It cannot be stressed strongly enough that social control of economic life—or, for that matter, any type of economic organization in an intricate industrial society—can function on a democratic basis only if it is based on civic education of the average man and woman in responsible participation in national and international affairs through the medium of public and private agencies. The term "education" is not used here in any formal sense, nor do we imply in the least that the rights of less educated citizens should be cut down. The main task, on the contrary, is to make those who have not had an opportunity to acquire either riches or formal knowledge become aware, along with other groups, of the necessity of keeping track of social developments and of taking an active part in them.

Such education for democratic action will make an effective supervisor of all government activities out of every man in the street, and it will perhaps be the most important guarantee of individual freedom under social control. If the man in the street keeps a watchful eye on any possible degeneration of social control into bureaucracy or dictatorship, if his political training enables him to dispose easily of quacks and demagogues, and if he talks sense in his daily discussions at home, at his working place, in his club or church, and on any other occasion, then the danger of any such degeneration will be greatly reduced.

Despite its importance, such individual action can constitute an effective guarantee of freedom only if it is complemented by a network of social organizations to channel and concentrate the feelings, wishes, and actions of the individual. Under any type of economic

setup, a modern democracy faces the following dilemma: on one hand, it requires a voluntary and effective organization of the various groups in order to make
the common people articulate and to take their actual
desires into full consideration. On the other hand, such
group organization, in our past experience, tends almost
inevitably to degenerate into a variety of pressure groups
and lobbies, which absorb much of the energy of legis-
lators and administrators. The dividing line between
a pressure lobby and a group representation of the
legitimate democratic type is not easy to define. The
only real yardstick is the extent to which such an organization takes into consideration the national and international effects of its suggestions and demands—that
is, whether or not it clamors for the fulfillment of its
claims regardless of possible harm to the rest of the
nation and perhaps the rest of the world; whether or
not it believes implicitly in the sacred right of, say, the
sugar growers or the teamsters or the dry-goods retailers
to have their special interests advanced no matter what
the cost of such a policy may be to the consumers, to
Uncle Sam, and to everyone else affected.

Democratic group organization might degenerate
into a mere rivalry of selfish pressure groups without
social understanding or responsibility. In this case the
difficulties and dangers involved would be no less serious
under social control of economic life than they have
been in a strictly competitive economy. The pressure
groups may force the controlling agencies to spend

much of their effort, not on building up efficient economy, but on warding off group attempts toward a one-sided monopolization of resources or policies. Inevitably these agencies would have to disregard some of the group demands in the interest of an integrated national policy, but they would, at the same time, be exposed to political pressures that would make such independence difficult and costly. In short, the combined pull of pressure groups in a multitude of divergent directions would threaten to tear national policy apart just as it does today.

What is really needed in a working democracy, under any type of economic institutions, is a civic education that would make group organizations conscious of their social responsibilities toward society as a whole, even while they duly represent the sectional needs of their members. Very often, indeed, the man in the street is far superior in social understanding to the leaders of his group organization, whose outlook may be obscured by lifelong professional advocacy of one policy or interest. The educational aim, in this case, is to induce the man in the street to keep a constant check on his leaders and to see to it that fresh blood is injected periodically into the veins of the representative body concerned.

If such social responsibility can be achieved—and some progress toward it has been made in recent decades in various western countries—then another important safeguard of freedom under social control will have

been established. Education for democratic action, to
be carried out both directly by the individual in his
community and by his group organization on a larger
scale, will provide a constant re-examination and criticism of all control policies and, thereby, an invaluable
guarantee of the "freedom to change."

Functional Representation

Among the functional groups in modern economic
life, the following deserve particular attention: consumers, labor, farmers, and small business. It would be
presumptuous to attempt here to advise each of them
how to behave. The best we can do is to point out some
differences in function.

The *consumers'* group, in the last analysis, includes
everybody. It is, however, its specific function in a controlled or an uncontrolled economy to see that the average individual derives the proper benefits from a
growing efficiency of production, that the production
program as a whole covers the actual needs of the consumer, and that the distributive and administrative
machinery does not absorb too many people and energies. In short, the consumers' body does not represent
any specific group of individuals as distinguished from
others; it is rather an organized emphasis upon certain
viewpoints and interests of everybody that might otherwise be obscured by the special interests of many people
in their additional capacities as producers, merchants,
wage earners, or administrators.

The *labor* group, represented by the trade-unions, will continue to defend the living standard of the wage earner and, especially, to strive for satisfactory wages and working conditions. However, a democratic control of economic life needs a far greater contribution from organized labor than that. It needs its active and constructive participation—as distinguished from mere interference—both in local plant management, especially through shop stewards with industrial and business training, and in national economic policy through a leadership with social responsibility and vision. It should trade the encouragement of greater labor productivity against the promise of economic security. The growth of such security will help eliminate narrow pressure-group approaches, for no social group has more to gain from a lasting success of democratic control than labor.

The co-operation of the *farmers*, in their double capacity as the producers of essentials and the largest group of self-employed people, will likewise be of key importance to the success of a controlled economy. In their own sphere, organized farmers have secured nearly everywhere a great deal of government control in their specific interest, especially in the form of tariffs, subsidies, and crop restrictions. Fluctuations in farm prices have traditionally been heavy, and the experience of 1929 and after, when a cyclical depression came on top of a postwar slump in world agriculture, is still very vivid.

Farm blocs in various parliaments have been powerful, and they have often used their influence in order
to obtain special advantages for the existing structure
of agriculture, to perpetuate vested interests, and to
prevent necessary changes in farming methods and
crops. On the other hand, great progress has been made
in the United States and some other countries in the
development of farm co-operatives, in rural electrifica-
tion and mechanization, and, above all, in general education in agricultural economics. Here again a sense
of greater security is very likely to reduce gradually the
old pressure-group mentality and to replace it by national and international responsibility in formulating
group demands and policies. The resourcefulness and
common sense of the farmer, focused in responsible
group action, can make a great contribution to a democratic pattern of economic control by organized society.

Small business, long both the pet and the dupe of
demagogues everywhere, has seldom been well organized. Moreover, its organizations have almost invariably
been engaged in constant skirmishes concerning the
right of each trade group to this or that type of business,
or in vain efforts to stem the tide of technological progress and to force a return to business conditions of the
past. This has been true of Europe even more than of
America. We can safely assume that small business will
survive in great numbers, especially in such fields as retail trade and the service industries, no matter which of
the control methods discussed receive emphasis. Cer-

tain lines of small business offer a substantial amount of knowledge and enterprise, and they present a valuable outlet for individual initiative. In other lines, no false sentimentality toward the "little fellow" should be allowed to serve as cloak for the subsidized preservation of outmoded business forms.

It is important to build up an organized and socially responsible representation of the small-business viewpoint, which would abandon both any reactionary pseudo-solution and the time-honored bickering about reserved hunting grounds for each business group. It should instead be ready and able to make a constructive contribution to economic control by a democratic society. As for big business, its private forms—especially private controls of a monopolistic character—will be greatly reduced by the reforms discussed. Those that survive need not be prodded into organized groupings, for the economic weight of big business has been expressed in powerful organizations for a long time; and on the basis of the past record little could be expected in the way of democratic safeguards from any private concentration of economic power.

To sum up, a variety of trustworthy safeguards of individual freedom under a socially controlled economy could and should be employed. There are convincing reasons to believe emphatically that the Bill of Rights can be applied as easily to a society that controls its economic development as to a society that lets it run amuck.

Political Safeguards

Free election of parliamentary bodies and their clean-cut authority to appoint and supervise the head controllers; continuance and expansion of civil liberties involving, above all, full freedom of opinion and criticism for every individual; and civic education for social participation and responsibility, which would apply both to individuals and to their organized representation in consumers', labor, farmers', and small-business groups—all these methods, and others that may be added, give sufficient assurance of individual freedom in a socially controlled economy.

CHAPTER VI

Economic Freedom in the Twentieth Century

MANY an ism that was convinced of its eternal validity turned out to be of passing significance only. After this discovery had been made, some of them went out of circulation; but many more adjusted themselves to new conditions and gradually changed their meaning beyond recognition, thus catering to the inertia of many a human mind.

Such semiconscious adaptation of principles and programs accounts for much of the existing confusion in our social and intellectual life. Some people go on using the old concepts in their original meaning, while others have adopted a new one. The result is that two or more people who use such terms as "Conservatism," "Liberalism," or "Socialism" often do not mean the same thing at all.

The original British concept of liberalism was almost identical with laissez faire. At the same time, British conservatism, which had its roots in precapitalist institutions and ideas, represented a paternalistic approach to economic society. In the United States, which developed without any comparable heritage of feudalism, those two concepts have practically been reversed in recent decades. In this country it is now conservatism which is usually identified with laissez-faire attitudes, except in connection with tariff policy. On the other hand, economic liberalism is now widely associated with a drive toward government controls for purposes of public welfare. Socialism, finally, means to some people Soviet communism, to others Nazism, and to still others a limited and evolutionary type of collectivism on the lines of the British Labour Party. In view of the Babylonic confusion of all these concepts today, it is more fruitful to discuss the issues at stake in terms of concrete policies than in those of isms, but the actual influence of broad ideological generalizations should not be underrated.

Social Systems Today

World society after the Second World War represents, in fact, a strange and unstable conglomerate of conservatism, fascism, liberalism, socialism, communism, and some other elements. Its lack of integration accounts for a great many of the troubles in which the victorious and the defeated nations alike—though in different degrees and forms—have found themselves involved. More particularly, this difference in social institutions and aims has overshadowed the early steps of the United Nations.

Hundreds of millions of people, especially in Asia, still live under precapitalist institutions, which, indeed, are melting away rapidly. North America stands as the lonely bulwark of capitalism, though its competitive features have gradually been reduced both by the concentration of economic power and by government intervention. The Soviet Union, at the other end of the scale, is developing an industrialized economy on a communist basis. Europe, greatly weakened as a whole, is somewhere between capitalism and socialism, and so are Australia and New Zealand. Latin America presents a mixture of feudal, capitalist, fascist, and socialist elements. The variations in living standards and socioeconomic philosophies are enormous, and all sectors of world society are in a process of flux. This process may change all standards and philosophies at a rapid pace and may easily make wealthy nations out of the beggars of today, and vice versa. It may also make various nations replace some of their traditional valuations by very different ones.

It is a world that, in one way or another, is out of tune with the expectations of all nineteenth-century thinkers. Industrialization has spread across the world and has swept away many old institutions in huge areas, but it has not removed the barriers of state sovereignty and has even strengthened them in some respects. The technological revolution has raised immeasurably the *potential* standard of living, but it has also contributed, in its immediate effects, to an increase in the sources of insecurity and to the severity of recurrent slumps. The social effects of modern science, industry, and urbanization have forced all nations to increase governmental intervention, instead of reducing it continuously as nineteenth-century liberalism had expected. John Stuart Mill's dream of world peace through free trade did not come true, both because free-trade policies turned out to be short-lived and because the roots of war were far more deeply embedded than in limitations to commercial intercourse only. National consciousness, itself a child of industrialism, degenerated into an aggressive nationalism on the political and economic levels, which led to continuous tensions and periodic conflicts. And with its failure to establish durable peace, the world sentenced itself to a state of permanent preparedness, which was bound to shatter the very basis of liberal hopes of the nineteenth-century type, namely, the competitive system itself.

With the growth of insecurity and frustration in a technologically advancing world, that peculiar and disgraceful feature of the twentieth century, Fascism, swept over most of Europe and parts of other continents. It grew fastest where feelings of national humiliation were strong for one reason or another; where the concentration of economic power had led to a monopolistic type of capitalism; where leading groups of business felt their privileges menaced by a strong labor

movement; where labor, business, farmers, handicraftsmen, and intellectuals alike were economically up-
rooted, especially in the wake of a heavy slump; and
where no firm democratic tradition existed.

The Fascist solution for economic insecurity was rearmament, and the ideological basis for this solution
was an aggressive nationalism that was bound to lead
to total war. It is true that the political and strategic
blunders made by the Axis dictators and their megalo-
maniac overrating of their own power led to an alliance
between their capitalist and anticapitalist opponents,
which cost the aggressors the war. Their intended victims, however, had a very close shave, and the Fascists,
despite their defeat, left enough poison in the organism
of the western world to bedevil its postwar adjustment
for quite a while ahead. Moreover, are all the western
nations safe from developing similar types of social
poison in case comparable sources of insecurity and
frustration should break through? We *wish* we could
answer with a definite Yes!

Was Marx Right?

The rise of Fascism in the middle of the twentieth
century caught most Marxians off guard no less than
it did their laissez-faire antagonists. To look in Marx'
books for all answers to the social issues that are at stake
today, eighty or one hundred years later, would hold
little promise for anyone. To confine oneself to the
scanty indications in these books concerning the con-

crete shape of postcapitalist society would be even less sensible. Yet the broad social discoveries of Marx and Engels deserve continued attention and possible integration with more recent patterns of research in economics, anthropology, psychology, and other fields, if a way out of the present chaos of world society is to be found.

The really great contribution of these thinkers was made in discovering, or rediscovering, the historical sequence of social systems. Such analysis replaced the timeless generalizations of the classical economists by concrete distinctions between slave society, feudalism, capitalism, and the expected socialist aftermath of capitalism. Marx also found that this process of constant change was determined mainly by a showdown of conflicting interests of social groups and classes. His concrete application of this theory of historical development led him to the conclusion that the social order of capitalism, like earlier class societies, had a limited lease of life. The socially conscious worker—expected to develop from the illiterate, exploited, animallike laborer of his day—was destined to play a decisive role in the emancipation of mankind, which Marx identified with the transition from capitalism to socialism.

Marx, however, made only statements of a very general character concerning the concrete shape of the socialist society that he saw ahead. There was no need for him to be more specific, for social conditions—that is, industrialization and the concentration of capital on the one hand and a development of proletarian class consciousness on the other—had first to ripen sufficiently before an actual transition to socialism could take place. The growth of an industrial reserve army as a result of ever more frequent and prolonged unemployment, a falling rate of average capital profit, a growing disproportion between producer goods' and consumer goods' industries resulting in periodic crises of increasing gravity, and other factors of disturbance would pave the way to an eventual expropriation of the expropriators by a class-conscious proletariat. Its transitional dictatorship (which, in Marx' own terminology, could quite well take place in the form of majority rule in an industrially ripe democracy) would lead to the ultimate end of class inequalities and of any oppressive state machinery.

While collective ownership of all means of production was clearly accepted as a general principle by Marx and his early followers, they failed, for the reason mentioned, to elaborate any concrete pattern of the economic transition to socialism or any specific picture of socialism itself. Any such attempt was looked upon for years as a vain utopianism that was unworthy of scientific socialism. As industrial capitalism developed and "ripened," other factors accounted for the continued reluctance of most Marxian socialists to specify the features of the collective economy to come.

First, labor organizations in many countries of western and central Europe, and in some other areas, had meanwhile acquired vested interests in the existing capitalist structure, without always being conscious of them. They had secured political rights, influence on many governmental agencies, a network of branches and locals, real estate, co-operative stores, camps, schools, welfare funds, and an extensive administrative machinery of their own. They retained less and less resemblance to the proletariat in the Communist Manifesto of 1848, which had "nothing to lose but its chains." In fact, they risked a great deal in getting involved in radical and possibly violent changes in the social structure—effects likely to result from any rapid collectivization or other interference with the set pattern of economic life.

Second, with the growing separation between ownership and management, the whole institution of property as applied to corporate enterprise had begun to lose or, at least, to change its economic significance. If tiny management groups at the top could control corporations and whole industries in a sovereign fashion without necessarily showing much concern for the wishes or interests of the thousands of ill-informed and inexpert absentee owners; if ownership in a world of holding companies and voting trusts had ceased to be the criterion or, at least, the symbol of actual control; if state intervention in or regulation of property rights had gradually changed the character of ownership itself—was sufficient reason left to regard a collectivization of all productive property as *the* solution for all social evils? Such questions usually remained outside the sphere of conscious consideration; but they influenced the labor and socialist movement indirectly, or they supplied it with an excuse for avoiding any radical action in the direction of collectivization, which still ranked prominently in its programs and platforms.

This does not necessarily mean that socialist "Revisionism" around the turn of the century, headed by Eduard Bernstein, was more up to date than its rival philosophy, orthodox Marxism under the leadership of Karl Kautsky. The Revisionists in Germany, under the influence of the traditional Prussian glorification of The State, believed that the government was developing into an impartial arbiter among the classes and that the antagonisms among them were thus on the decline. Only incidentally did they support a limited and gradual pattern of collectivization, and they paid little attention to the concrete social forces that were to dominate such a collectivistic state. A few decades later, indeed, the Russian Revolution, with its complete expropriation of the old ruling classes and its collectivization of all means of production, seemed to cut through any doubts concerning the continuing significance of ownership in modern society.

Yet the example of the Soviet economy, in its property aspects as well as in many others, was not applicable to western industrialism. Expropriation in Russia had attacked a semifeudal agrarianism upon which a few centers of highly concentrated, largely foreign-owned industry had been superimposed. Moreover, the old Tsarist absolutism had collapsed completely in the wake of a military defeat, and a completely new type of authoritarian government had followed.

In the western countries, with their long and continuous processes of governmental administration along democratic lines and with their widely distributed, domestically owned industry, conditions were very different. In these countries competitive capitalism had developed on a broader economic basis, and the capitalist spirit had permeated many more social groups and institutions than in Russia. At the same time, private concentration of economic power had gained ground, and a distinct threat of industrial monopolies had arisen. The western countries had not accepted the central European pattern of financial control by bank concerns over industry; they had not confined themselves to foreign-controlled islands of capitalist industry on Russian lines; their industrialism was less state-fostered than that of other areas; but they had developed strong barriers to effective competition through the omnivorous process of competition itself.

A cry for government intervention came from those who were concerned about the future of competition unless a rigorous guardian watched constantly over the rules of the game and their enforcement. They were joined by those who were increasingly worried about the social effects of industrialism, with its cyclical fluctuations in business activity. The rise of the labor movement had resulted in limitations on downward wage adjustments in a depression, the practice that had been the traditional answer of business to the cycle; and the price of labor had become even less flexible than the prices of many other commodities. The development of a conscious guidance of the credit market by the banks of issue, including after 1913 the Federal Reserve System in the United States, had opened up new avenues through which the constant threat of periodic depressions could be attacked, though many people continued to consider any such thought as dangerous.

Finally, the crucial impact of preparedness and war in the machine age, culminating in the atomic threat, forced even governments and business groups with a strong philosophy of laissez faire to adopt interventionism on a growing scale, as a matter of life or death. Laissez faire retained some influence as an abstract philosophy of economic behavior, or else as an object of wishful thinking. In actual economic policy, both the growing support for interventionism in business circles and a more discriminating attitude toward collectivism on the part of labor had paved the way to a novel combination that is best characterized by the name of John Maynard Keynes.

The Scope of Keynesian Economics

Keynes' economic philosophy, in its developed form, was clearly a product of one of the greatest shocks from which world capitalism had ever suffered, one second only to the Russian Revolution: the great depression. The social impossibility of any further reliance on an eventual cure through the market automatism (to the limited extent that it was still in operation), the severe danger from mass unemployment to democracy and peace, the partial success of the New Deal, and other experiences of the early thirties formed the general background against which Keynes' *General Theory of Employment, Interest and Money* was written. When it was published in 1936, the attention that it received could not be fully explained by its intrinsic qualities. Its role as an ingenious summary and interpretation of the disastrous economic experience that the capitalist world had just gone through was of no less importance. It is true that a decade earlier, in his famous essay on "The End of Laissez-Faire," Mr. Keynes had given some indication of the worries that had befallen him while a disciple of the liberal Cambridge School and of his search for working correctives of a competitive mechanism.

This is not the place to describe the Keynesian system of economics in any detail. Its starting point is in a criticism of the classical law of markets. This law implies a necessary tendency in a competitive economy toward an equilibrium (specifically definable) among investment, consumption, and employment. Keynes is anxious to show that such an equilibrium can exist on various levels of employment. Under conditions which are more frequent than not, entrepreneurs can expect profit to reach its maximum level with employment far from full. Generally the volume of employment depends on investment and thus, indirectly, on the entrepreneur's inducement to invest. The latter, in turn, is influenced by the marginal efficiency of capital, which, through the medium of interest rates, is closely related to the prevailing preference for liquidity and to the quantity of money in circulation. At the same time, investment decisions are limited by the expected propensity to consume, translated into effective demand. In the last analysis, therefore, investment and the employment involved depend on the extent of money income that is expected to be spent for consumption in a broad sense. For psychological reasons, the propensity to consume of an industrially advanced population does not necessarily keep pace with the need to create employment. This propensity is insufficient to encourage an amount of investment that would provide the employment opportunities required—unless certain correctives, especially in the field of monetary and income policy, are applied. In Keynes' own words,

The State will have to exercise a guiding influence on the propensity to consume partly through its scheme of taxation, partly by fixing the rate of interest, and partly, perhaps, in other ways. Furthermore, it seems unlikely that the influence of banking policy on the rate of interest will be sufficient by itself to determine an optimum rate of investment. I conceive, therefore, that a somewhat comprehensive socialization of investment will prove the only means of securing an approximation to full employment; though this need not exclude all manner of compromises and of devices by which public authority will co-operate with private initiative. But beyond this no obvious case is made out for a system of State Socialism which would embrace most of the economic life of the community. It is not the ownership of the instruments of production which is important for the State to assume. If the State is able to determine the aggregate amount of resources devoted to augmenting the instruments and the basic rate of reward to those who own them, it will have accomplished all that is necessary. Moreover, the necessary measures of socialization can be introduced gradually and without a break in the general traditions of society. . . .

The central controls necessary to ensure full employment will, of course, involve a large extension of the traditional functions of government. Furthermore, the modern classical theory has itself called attention to various conditions in which the free play of economic forces may need to be curbed or guided. But there will still remain a wide field for the exercise of private initiative and responsibility. Within this field the traditional advantages of individualism will still hold good. . . .

It is certain that the world will not much longer tolerate the unemployment which, apart from brief intervals of excitement, is associated—and, in my opinion, inevitably associated—with present-day capitalistic individualism. But it may be possible by a right analysis of the problem to cure the disease whilst preserving efficiency and freedom.[1]

Keynes' conclusions, to be exact, do not involve any comprehensive pattern of social control or planning, or do so only implicitly. What he really suggests is the con-

---

[1] *Op. cit.*, pp. 378–381, quoted by permission of the publisher, Harcourt, Brace and Company.

scious use of governmental powers, especially those of the monetary and fiscal type, to keep private enterprise on an even keel and to develop certain correctives to competition, designed to achieve the full-employment type of economic equilibrium. He has certainly succeeded in exploding the orthodox belief in a pre-established harmony between high profit and high employment or low wages and high employment, and in reminding his contemporaries of the basic fact that people's income—that from wages in particular—means not only producer cost but consumer outlays. He probably, however, overrates the influence of purely monetary manipulation, especially that of interest rates, upon prosperity in general and employment in particular; he gives no real quantitative analysis of the relationship between changes in outlays and changes in employment; and he pays little attention to the effects of *general* insecurity in contemporary society—the constant fear of depression, technology, group conflicts, war, and of the future in general—upon both the private inducement to invest and the changing propensity to consume. Finally, he gives little indication of any real belief in a preventive and constructive type of social control.

His opposite number in the United States, Alvin H. Hansen, places particular emphasis on the idea of "compensatory" spending, that is, on that type of government intervention that is applied only when and if private outlays lag behind the requirements of full employment. Although this theory, a restated version of Keynesianism, recognizes the periodic necessity for the government to bring private business back on an even keel, it is in a sense the negation of any comprehensive control or general planning in advance by organized society. It is true that Hansen has also elaborated with great care certain *special* aspects of economic planning, such as urban and regional redevelopment, and that he has done so with particular attention to fields in which compensatory spending is likely to have the most beneficial effects upon employment.

At any rate, the great depression appears to have struck a deadly blow at the classical assumption of a steady tendency toward an all-round social equilibrium in the competitive process. Keynes not only felt that at least a periodic corrective was necessary, he also rediscovered the identity, in an industrialized economy with relatively high living standards, of the wage earners with the largest group of consumers—an identity that had been neglected by most of the classical economists and their marginal-utility descendants.

Strangely enough, it had not been elaborated in any detail by Marx either. A whole generation of economists had been brought up in the tradition of the subsistence theory and its "iron law" of wages, and believed in an inevitable impoverishment of the working class. It would have been difficult for that generation, therefore, either to perceive the leading role of the working class as a consumer or to admit any real possibility of improving its living standard under capitalism. In this particular sense—which should not be overrated—Keynes is more "radical" than Marx, for he supplies, under certain conditions, a more direct incentive for immediate action on the part of organized labor in the interest not only of higher wages but of higher employment as well. Keynes believes, to be sure, that "the struggle about money wages primarily affects the distribution of the aggregate real wage between different labor groups," while the *general* level of wages depends chiefly on the monetary policy adopted. "Thus it is fortunate that the workers, though unconsciously, are instinctively more reasonable economists than the classical school, inasmuch as they resist reductions of money wages . . . whereas they do not resist reductions of real wages." [2] In short, organized labor does not ordinarily prevent an economic adjustment through price fluctuations; at the same time, its action may have the aggregate effect of encouraging an adequate flow of money in a critical business situation.

This is not the place to discuss the merits of Keynes' argument in general. In a way, he offers a more hopeful outlook than either the classical school or Marx for the workers' standard of living under capitalism, provided indeed that certain correctives are employed. Implicitly this means, of course, that this system is not nearly so much beyond repair for Keynes as it is for Marx; instead

---

[2] *Op. cit.*, pp. 14 f.

of overthrowing it altogether Keynes suggests patching it up whenever necessary.

From a different point of view, recent analysis of imperfect competition has likewise underlined the *intrinsic* limitations that are set to any market automatism, not to mention its historical limitations. Such analysis has thus suggested the use of correctives by organized society. This is the implication both of Joan Robinson's *Economics of Imperfect Competition* and of Edward Chamberlin's *Theory of Monopolistic Competition,* two books that discuss in a formal, timeless way the monopolistic influences that generally result from such factors as the varying elasticity of supply and demand, the size and location of firms, the limits of market information, and the highly diversified character of wants and goods. Other authors, like Thurman W. Arnold and Corwin D. Edwards, have emphasized the recent concentration of economic power and the actual range of monopolistic practices in American and international business in our period, without drawing any policy conclusions save those pointing in the direction of government aids to small business.

Twentieth-Century Liberalism

From two opposite directions, therefore, the gap between one wing of socialism and one wing of procapitalism has been narrowed, though it remains considerable. The former group is now prepared to accept various types and degrees of social control instead of insisting on the collectivization of *all* productive property; the latter group now admits the necessity of public controls, at least to the extent that private enterprise fails to maintain a general economic equilibrium on a socially desirable level.

All this means that the nineteenth-century concept of liberalism—that of laissez faire—has now become a tenet of conservatism, and in some respects of reaction. The heritage of liberalism, in its more fundamental meaning, has now been taken over by those who recognize that neither the freedom aims nor the welfare hopes of the early nineteenth century can actually be achieved without purposeful action by a democratically organized society. The marriage of liberalism and socialism, of individual freedom and social control, may look at first like a *mésalliance* to the intellectual parents on both sides, and the mutual adjustment cannot avoid some initial difficulties; yet such a combination presents in western society the only real hope for our generation.

It would clearly differ from both state capitalism and state socialism. State capitalism organizes private enterprise in a structure of combines, trade associations, and cartels—a structure operated primarily in the interest of private capital groups by their own representatives in the government. State socialism is a centralized system of nationalized enterprises to be operated by a benevolent bureaucracy in the presumed interest of public welfare. Both methods neglect at least one of the two essentials that have been pointed out, namely, either the greatest possible control of society or the greatest possible freedom of the individual.

The yardstick of public welfare, which has just been mentioned, is of course exposed to controversy in its actual economic applications. Differences of opinion will often arise concerning the benefit or prejudice of a concrete policy to specific groups. Attempts by A. C. Pigou, Colin Clark, and others to define economic welfare in terms of abundant supply of all goods and services that are customarily exchanged for money have not been entirely convincing. In public policy other social yardsticks inevitably come into the picture, too— health, education, and art, for instance—and the borderline between them and strictly material yardsticks is often vague. This merely shows that value judgments cannot be entirely avoided in determining just what constitutes public welfare. Final judgment on this issue must be left, in the last resort, to the normal processes of free democratic discussion, just as it is today whenever similar decisions are required.

On purely economic grounds, J. R. Hicks and others have expressed doubts whether either individual or group levels of welfare could be compared at all. If this were literally true, then economic analysis loses much of its *raison d'être*. However, as A. P. Lerner has pointed out, a quantitative sample of adequate size could indicate sufficiently the probable requirements for equal levels of welfare. In other words, while a comparison of two isolated individuals would be pretty difficult, a

comparison of welfare levels on a br̶...
quite possible; and it takes place all
decisions of public policy today. In sho̶r̶t̶,
choices, in defining economic welfare and in determining the control methods that lead to it, may include
a certain element of arbitrariness; but so does every
decision—whether active or passive—of public policy.
Certainly the problems that are implicit in the concrete
definition of economic welfare do not constitute a case
against social control as such.

In our day, lack of social control over the economic
forces means periodic misery and constant insecurity;
insecurity means frustration, aggressiveness, and war;
and the mere possibility of war means a quasi-
totalitarian regimentation in "peacetime" and the end
of freedom sooner or later. The impact of modern
science in its potential of both productivity and destruc-
tiveness is such that lack of social control, in its final
result, means lack of individual freedom as well. There
is, in fact, some danger that "liberal" economists today
may go on fighting the *last* depression, just like those
proverbial generals who always prepare for the last war.
If international insecurity should continue, then the
main problems facing economists will not be depression
and unemployment, but inflation and a distorted structure and location of industries vainly attempting to cope
with economic implications of the atomic threat. Freedom in this case will be jeopardized by a warlike dis-

tortion of social control rather than by its absence.

We cannot here go very deeply into the philosophical concept of freedom in general. Certainly it should not be confused with anarchy. Woodrow Wilson, in *The New Freedom*, says that "human freedom consists in perfect adjustments of human interests and human activities and human energies." Others, like Herman Finer, have emphasized economic welfare as an essential factor in freedom. Georges Clemenceau saw the essence of freedom in self-discipline to the point where one takes necessary restrictions for granted. Still others regard tolerance toward nonconformism as the real indicator of freedom or measure the freedom content of social innovations in terms of whether there is a legitimate "way back."

At any rate, what really matters is the integrated understanding by the man in the street of natural and social necessities. Such understanding will determine how soon the vital adjustment of obsolete concepts in economics to twentieth-century requirements is made. This adjustment will be successful only if we realize at the same time that neither social control nor economic planning can be a self-purpose. They are, in the final analysis, modern devices designed to help develop the *individual* by giving him a "basic ration" of security and a reasonably good chance, as far as objective factors are concerned, to develop his socio-economic position.

The goal of economic security itself cannot be taken for granted yet. Moreover, it requires careful determination. A substantial sector of business and some other groups still believe that the threat of unemployment is necessary to keep workers from loafing, or that depressions are a kind of spring cleaning that periodically weeds out inefficient business units. They consider insecurity as both inevitable and fundamentally healthy. Whether or not any social group today has a genuine interest in economic insecurity, it should be clear after the interwar experience that the vast majority of an industrial population has the opposite interest.

This leaves the question of *how much* economic security society as a whole should aim at. Undoubtedly a conflict may arise between the goal of security and that of progress if the former is mistakenly identified with either stagnation or the indiscriminate preservation of all vested interests. Security should, however, be identified with social control of the rate and direction of progress, not with the absence of progress. It is perfectly true that the aim of economic security should not be allowed to crush that of productive efficiency. In its importance for social welfare, the total result of the latter will continue, for a long time to come, to exceed the promotion of economic equality, though there is no intrinsic necessity of conflict between these two aims.

In short, security should not be misinterpreted as a guarantee of a good life for every individual regardless of his own conduct. It should rather be thought of as the constant provision, by organized society, of a sufficient number of opportunities for personal (not necessarily financial) development in relation to the number of individuals who look for them. Sir William Beveridge has warned against distorting his full-employment plan into a belief that any individual could choose to be an Archbishop of Canterbury. Economic security cannot mean a guarantee of any specific job for any one individual. It can mean a guarantee against unemployment as a mass occurrence, a guarantee of sufficient educational opportunities for those interested in occupational advancement, and a number of related policies. Even F. A. Hayek, while arguing against "restrictive security," appears to approve of "security against severe physical privation, the certainty of a given minimum of sustenance for all," though he has very little to say on what to do about it positively.

It should also be clear that both economic security and social control far exceed in scope the goal of "full employment." In the first place, totalitarian regimes have achieved full employment, too, but in a manner unacceptable to western populations. Second, the term "full employment" is sometimes used in economic literature in a purely formal sense, "as a statistical norm, with which states of employment that have existed, do exist, or might be made to exist can be compared. . . ." [3] Even if, in using this concept, we allow for an irreducible core of unemployment in practice,

---

[3] A. C. Pigou, *Lapses From Full Employment* (London, 1945), p. 2. See also Oxford Institute of Statistics, *The Economics of Full Employment* (Oxford, 1945).

the social and economic content of the concept still needs careful definition. Third, such a definition must take into account the wage level, the degree of mobility of labor, and the extent of employment of physical resources as essentials for judgment of any concrete program for full employment. Fourth, full employment, in the absence of further definition, may or may not refer to the abolition not only of the cyclical type of unemployment, but of the structural, technological, seasonal, and other types as well. Fifth, concrete programs for full employment are ordinarily concerned at best with moderate correctives to a competitive mechanism, such as public investment or the redistribution of incomes. Not very often are they integrated with the broader aspects of social control, such as industrial structure, the welfare of underprivileged groups, civic responsibility, political and other freedoms, international co-operation, and cultural values.

All this is said, not in order to discount the concept or goal of full employment, but in order to place it in its proper setting, namely, as one important aspect of the broader aims of economic security and social control.

These aims, we expect, will gradually be built into a more general setting of those social and ethical values that most of us would recognize as valid for our generation. And since we live in one world, everything depends on whether sufficient agreement among the nations of the world can be achieved on these values and their practical implementation, and on whether a working international co-ordination of national control policies can be secured until the whole concept of national sovereignty can finally be dumped where it belongs, into the junkyard of obsolete ideas.

Neither a final stabilization of society in a stationary millennium nor an early equalization of world socio-economic systems needs to be expected in order to believe that a development toward economic security, rising standards of living, a wise combination of social control and individual initiative, and international co-operation among nations with a different structure of society are policies both possible and imperative in our day.

After discovering the strength of irrational factors in individuals and nations alike, most of us, indeed, are no longer inclined to share the rosy-cheeked optimism of earlier generations concerning an *inevitable* trend toward social progress. Nor is this whole discussion meant to make us overlook those elements of personal insecurity that are due to noneconomic causes. After eliminating, in the incidence of personal insecurity today, all those factors resulting from concrete social conditions, a hard core of purely individual disturbances will remain. However, insecurity will then be a problem for psychotherapists only and not for social scientists or statesmen.

The recognition of the impact of nonmaterial drives and values may lead eventually to greater realism and more purposeful effort toward such progress. At the moment, however, social control in general still faces the barrier that, on a more local scale, was drastically described in a *Fortune* article on "The Traffic Outrage" (October, 1946): "Those who suffer from traffic congestion in New York City face a maddening truth: although their pain can be relieved, it will probably go on indefinitely." One need not share such pessimism in order to realize the magnitude of social education still necessary.

Whether we place the main emphasis on the element of planning or of control—and the two concepts, we repeat, are not necessarily identical—whether our starting point is in material or in ethical considerations, and whether it is in the element of individual initiative or in that of socialist collectivism, the western pattern of an economic program today should combine the following principles:

First, the over-all responsibility of organized society to keep the development and fluctuations of economic life under control—a task that far exceeds both the mere provision of a formal framework for government regulation on traditional lines and the mere prosecution of gross abuses of economic power. It will include substantial changes in property relations without neglecting other, more indirect methods of social control.

Second, individual initiative in carrying out such controls or plans in concrete detail and on the local level, with substantial use of money rewards in various forms, including profit in those fields where private enterprise is preserved; selective use of incentive pay and taxation; and, generally, the greatest amount of decentralized responsibility that is compatible with an integrated national policy.

Third, international co-ordination of national controls to prevent mutual impediments, whether intended or not, to the cause of economic progress. Such co-ordination will be an effective and indispensable step toward a gradual elimination of outmoded concepts of national sovereignty. It will thus help reduce the constant threat of total war, which may otherwise engulf any social progress that has been made.

Such principles of applied welfare economics should be acceptable to all those whose stake in a healthy society exceeds that in special privileges or vested interests, and that is the great majority of the population in every country. The fundamental importance of individual freedom and initiative has been increasingly recognized by socialists in western countries and some other parts of the world. At the same time, many whose starting point was purely individualistic begin to realize the necessity today of social control over our material development. Both of these trends point to an integration of these currents in a new liberal socialism. It will differ in various respects from that particular pattern of socialism that Karl Marx had in mind almost a century ago; but it will remain his historic merit to have grasped and stressed the general necessity and possibility of social control over economic forces.

It would be futile to believe in any pre-established or intrinsic identity of all group interests in this direction. Social progress can seldom be achieved without a heavy fight against privileges, vested interests, and plain stupid ignorance. Yet those who have a vital stake in an economic society fit for our generation to live in represent an ever-growing majority, and some of those who ordinarily might stick to their privileges regardless of their social consequences are beginning to realize that individual wealth or power may be of very little use if a social earthquake shatters the very basis on which it rests.

Those twin scourges of our generation, insecurity and war, affect more people today than ever before. In an atomic explosion there is little discrimination between a palatial mansion and a rotten slum. Mankind has chosen to learn its lessons the hard way, and very little time is left to learn them. How much longer will there be?

Selected Bibliography

American Economic Association, *Readings in the Social Control of Industry* (Philadelphia, 1942).

Amonn, Alfred, *Konkurrenz und Planwirtschaft* (Berne, 1946).

Angell, Sir Norman, *Why Freedom Matters* (Harmondsworth, 1940).

——, *The Steep Places* (New York, 1947).

Anshen, Ruth N., ed., *Freedom: Its Meaning* (New York, 1940).

——, ed., *Our Emergent Civilization* (New York, 1947).

Ascoli, M., and Lehmann, F., ed., *Political and Economic Democracy* (New York, 1937).

Ayres, C. E., *The Divine Right of Capital* (Boston, 1944).

——, *The Theory of Economic Progress* (Chapel Hill, 1944).

Baker, John R., *Science and the Planned State* (New York, 1945).

Baldwin, Claude D., *Economic Planning: Its Aims and Implications* (Urbana, Ill., 1942).

Ballinger, Willis J., *By Vote of the People* (New York, 1946).

Bauer, Otto, *Zwischen zwei Weltkriegen: Die Krise der Weltwirtschaft, der Demokratie und des Sozialismus* (Bratislava, 1936).

Becker, Carl L., *Freedom and Responsibility in the American Way of Life* (New York, 1945).

Belloc, Hilaire, *The Servile State* (New York, 1946).

Belshaw, Horace, *Recovery Measures in New Zealand: A Comparison With the New Deal in the United States* (Wellington, N.Z., 1936).

Berkovits, Eugen, *The Key to Full Employment Without Regimentation* (New York, 1945).

Berle, A., and Means, G. C., *The Modern Corporation and Private Property* (New York, 1932).

Bettelheim, Charles, *Les Problèmes théoriques et pratiques de la planification* (Paris, 1946).

Beveridge, Sir William H., *Full Employment in a Free Society* (New York, 1945).

Bingham, Alfred M., *The Practice of Idealism* (New York, 1944).

——, *Man's Estate: Adventures in Economic Discovery* (New York, 1939).

Bloch, Ernst, *Freiheit und Ordnung* (New York, 1946).

Borgese, G. A., *Common Cause* (New York, 1943).

Bowles, Chester, *Tomorrow Without Fear* (New York, 1946).

Brookings Institution, *Government and Economic Life* (Washington, 1939–1940), 2 vols.

Bryn-Jones, David, *Toward a Democratic New Order* (Minneapolis, 1945).

Bureau d'Etudes Sociales (Belgium), *L'Exécution du plan du travail* (Antwerp, 1935).

Burnham, James, *The Managerial Revolution* (New York, 1941).

Carr, Edward H., *Conditions of Peace* (New York, 1942).

——, *The Soviet Impact on the Western World* (New York, 1947).

Chase, Stuart, *For This We Fought* (New York, 1946).

Clark, Colin, *The Conditions of Economic Progress* (London, 1940).

——, *The Economics of 1960* (London, 1942).

Clark, John M., *Social Control of Business* (New York, 1939).

——, *Alternative to Serfdom* (New York, 1948).

Cochran, T. C., and Miller, W., *The Age of Enterprise* (New York, 1942).

Cole, G. D. H., *Economic Planning* (New York, 1935).

——, *The Intelligent Man's Guide to the Post-War World* (New York, 1948).

——, *The Machinery of Socialist Planning* (London, 1938).

——, *The Means to Full Employment* (London, 1943).

——, *Socialism in Evolution* (Harmondsworth, 1938).

Condliffe, J. B., and Stevenson, A., *The Common Interest in International Economic Organisation* (Montreal, 1944).

Copland, Douglas B., *The Road to High Employment* (Cambridge, Mass., 1945).

Corey, Lewis, *Unfinished Task* (New York, 1942).

Cousins, Norman, *Modern Man Is Obsolete* (New York, 1945).

Dewey, E. R., and Dakin, E. F., *Cycles: The Science of Prediction* (New York, 1947).

Dewey, John, *Freedom and Culture* (New York, 1939).

——, *Problems of Men* (New York, 1946).

Dickinson, H. D., *Economics of Socialism* (London, 1939).

Dieterlen, P., *Au delà du capitalisme* (Paris, 1946).

Dobb, Maurice, *Political Economy and Capitalism* (London, 1937).

Drucker, Peter F., *The End of Economic Man* (New York, 1939).

——, *The Future of Industrial Man* (New York, 1942).

Ebenstein, William, ed., *Man and the State* (New York, 1947).

Eldridge, Seba, *Development of Collective Enterprise* (Lawrence, Kan., 1943).

Elfenbein, Hiram, *Socialism From Where We Are* (New York, 1945).

Ezekiel, Mordecai, *Jobs for All Through Industrial Expansion* (New York, 1939).

——, ed., *Towards World Prosperity* (New York, 1947).

Fergusson, Harvey, *People and Power* (New York, 1947).

Finer, Herman, *Road to Reaction* (Boston, 1945).

Fisher, A. G. B., *Economic Progress and Social Security* (London, 1945).

——, *International Implications of Full Employment in Great Britain* (London and New York, 1946).

Fitch, Lyle, ed., *Planning for Jobs* (Philadelphia, 1946).

Frank, Sir Oliver, *Central Planning and Control in War and Peace* (Cambridge, Mass., 1947).

Fromm, Erich, *Escape From Freedom* (New York, 1941).

Galloway, George B., and associates, *Planning for America* (New York, 1941).

Ginzberg, Eli, *The Illusion of Economic Stability* (New York, 1939).

Glenday, Roy G., *The Future of Economic Society* (London, 1944).

Gollancz, Victor, *Our Threatened Values* (London, 1946).

Gordon, Manya, *How to Tell Progress From Reaction* (New York, 1944).

Graham, Frank D., *Social Goals and Economic Institutions* (Princeton, 1942).

Gurvitch, Georges, *The Bill of Social Rights* (New York, 1945).

Halévy, Elie, *L'Ere des tyrannies* (Paris, 1938).

Hall, Robert L., *The Economic System in a Socialist State* (London, 1937).

Hansen, Alvin H., *Economic Policy and Full Employment* (New York, 1947).

Selected Bibliography

——, *Fiscal Policy and Business Cycles* (New York, 1941).

Harris, Seymour E., ed., *The New Economics: Keynes' Influence on Theory and Public Policy* (New York, 1947).

Hayek, F. A., *The Road to Serfdom* (Chicago, 1944).

——, ed., *Collectivist Economic Planning* (London, 1935).

Hayes, Harry G., *Spending, Saving and Employment* (New York, 1945).

Hazlitt, Henry, *Economics in One Lesson* (New York, 1947).

Heimann, Eduard, *Freedom and Order* (New York, 1947).

Hewes, Thomas, *Decentralize for Liberty* (New York, 1947).

Huxley, Aldous, *Science, Liberty and Peace* (New York, 1946).

Huxley, Julian, *On Living in a Revolution* (New York, 1942).

International Labour Office, *Public Investment and Full Employment* (Montreal, 1946).

Jaeger, Muriel, *Liberty Versus Equality* (London, 1943).

Kaplan, A. D. H., *The Guarantee of Annual Wages* (Washington, 1947).

Klein, Lawrence R., *The Keynesian Revolution* (New York, 1947).

Keynes, J. M., *The End of Laissez-Faire* (London, 1927).

——, *General Theory of Unemployment, Interest and Money* (New York, 1936).

Knight, Frank H., *The Ethics of Competition* (New York, 1935).

——, *Freedom and Reform* (New York, 1947).

Koestler, Arthur, *The Yogi and the Commissar* (New York, 1945).

Laidler, Harry W., *A Program for Modern America* (New York, 1936).

Landauer, Karl, *Theory of National Economic Planning* (Berkeley, Calif., 1944).

Lange, Oscar, *On the Economic Theory of Socialism*, ed. by B. E. Lippincott (Minneapolis, 1938).

——, *Price Flexibility and Employment* (Bloomington, Ind., 1944).

Laski, Harold J., *Liberty in the Modern State* (New York, 1930).

Lasswell, Harold D., *World Politics and Personal Insecurity* (New York, 1935).

——, *World Politics Faces Economics* (New York, 1945).

Lauterbach, Albert, *Economics in Uniform: Military Economy and Social Structure* (Princeton, 1943).

League of Nations, *Economic Stability in the Postwar World* (Geneva, 1945).

Lerner, Abba P., *The Economics of Control* (New York, 1944).

Lerner, A. P., and Graham, F. D., *Planning and Paying for Full Employment* (Princeton, 1946).

Lippmann, Walter, *An Inquiry Into the Principles of the Good Society* (Boston, 1937).

Loeb, Harold, *Full Production Without War* (Princeton, 1946).

Lorwin, Lewis L., *Time for Planning* (New York, 1945).

Lynch, David, *The Concentration of Economic Power* (New York, 1946).

Lynd, Robert S., *Knowledge for What?* (Princeton, 1939).

Mackenzie, Findlay, ed., *Planned Society: Yesterday, Today, Tomorrow* (New York, 1937).

Man, Henri de, *Réflexions sur l'économie dirigée* (Paris and Brussels, 1932).

Mannheim, Karl, *Diagnosis of Our Time* (New York, 1944).

——, *Man and Society in an Age of Reconstruction* (New York, 1940).

Mayo, Elton, *The Social Problems of an Industrial Civilization* (Boston, 1945).

Selected Bibliography

Meade, J. E., and Hitch, C. J., *An Introduction to Economic Analysis and Policy* (New York, 1946).

Mill, John Stuart, *On Liberty* (New York, 1926).

——, *On Social Freedom* (New York, 1941).

Mises, Ludwig, *Bureaucracy* (New Haven, 1944).

——, *Socialism: An Economic and Sociological Analysis* (London, 1936).

Mitchell, Broadus, *Depression Decade: From New Era Through New Deal 1929–41* (New York, 1947).

Morrison, Herbert S., and associates, *Can Planning Be Democratic?* (London, 1944).

Mossé, Robert, *L'Economie collectiviste* (Paris, 1939).

Moszkowska, Natalie, *Zur Dynamik des Spätkapitalismus* (Zurich, 1945).

Mumford, Lewis, *Faith for Living* (New York, 1940).

Nathan, Robert R., *Mobilizing for Abundance* (New York, 1944).

Ohlin, Bertil, ed., *Social Problems and Policies in Sweden* (Annals of the American Academy of Political and Social Science, vol. 197; Philadelphia, 1938).

Ortega y Gasset, José, *Concord and Liberty* (New York, 1946).

Orton, William A., *The Liberal Tradition* (New Haven, 1945).

O'Shaughnessy, Michael J., *Economic Democracy and Private Enterprise* (New York, 1945).

Oxford Institute of Statistics, *The Economics of Full Employment* (Oxford, 1945).

Pareto, Vilfredo, *The Mind and Society* (New York, 1935), vol. IV.

Pierson, John H. G., *Full Employment and Free Enterprise* (Washington, 1947).

Pigou, A. C., *Lapses From Full Employment* (London, 1945).

——, *Socialism Versus Capitalism* (London, 1937).

Polanyi, Karl, *The Great Transformation* (New York, 1944).

Polanyi, Michael, *Full Employment and Free Trade* (Cambridge, Eng., 1945).

——, *Science, Faith and Society* (London, 1946).

Raudenbush, David W., *Democratic Capitalism* (New York, 1946).

Raymond, Fred, *The Limitist* (New York, 1947).

Richberg, Donald, *Government and Business Tomorrow* (New York, 1943).

Robbins, Lionel, *Economic Planning and International Order* (London, 1937).

Robinson, Joan, *An Essay on Marxian Economics* (London, 1942).

Rodgers, Cleveland, *American Planning* (New York, 1947).

Roepke, Wilhelm, *Civitas Humana: Grundfragen der Gesellschafts- und Wirtschaftsreform* (Erlenbach-Zurich, 1944).

Ruml, Beardsley, *Government, Business and Values* (New York, 1945).

Schumpeter, Joseph A., *Capitalism, Socialism and Democracy* (2d ed., New York, 1947).

Simons, Henry C., *Economic Policy for a Free Society* (Chicago, 1948).

Soule, George, *The Future of Liberty* (New York, 1936).

——, *Prosperity Decade: From War to Depression, 1917–29* (Cambridge, Mass., 1947).

——, *The Strength of Nations* (New York, 1942).

Staley, Eugene, *World Economy in Transition* (New York, 1939).

——, *World Economic Development* (Montreal, 1944).

Sternberg, Fritz, *The Coming Crisis* (New York, 1947).

Strachey, John, *The Theory and Practice of Socialism* (New York, 1936).

Selected Bibliography

Sturmthal, Adolf, *The Tragedy of European Labor* (New York, 1943).

Swanson, E. W., and Schmidt, E. P., *Economic Stagnation or Progress?* (New York, 1946).

Sweezy, Paul M., *The Theory of Capitalist Development* (New York, 1942).

Tawney, R. H., *The Acquisitive Society* (London, 1926).

Terborgh, George, *The Bogey of Economic Maturity* (Chicago, 1945).

U.S. Senate, Special Committee to Study and Survey Problems of Small Business Enterprises, *Economic Concentration and World War II* (Washington, 1946).

U.S. Senate, Subcommittee of the Committee on Banking and Currency, Hearings, *Full Employment Act of 1945* (Washington, 1945).

Veblen, Thorstein, *The Theory of Business Enterprise* (New York, 1912).

Voigt, F. A., *Unto Caesar* (New York, 1938).

Walker, E. Ronald, *From Economic Theory to Policy* (Chicago, 1943).

Wallace, Henry A., *Sixty Million Jobs* (New York, 1945).

Wilson, Woodrow, *The New Freedom* (New York, 1914).

Wootton, Barbara, *Freedom Under Planning* (Chapel Hill, 1945).

——, *Plan or No Plan* (New York, 1935).

Wright, David McC., *The Economics of Disturbance* (New York, 1947).

——, *Democracy and Progress* (New York, 1948).

Zweig, Ferdynand, *The Planning of Free Societies* (London, 1942).

Index